English Progress

Pupil Book 2
Levels 4-6

Series editor: **Geoff Barton**
Series consultant: **Michael Jones**

Authors: **Claire Austin-Macrae**
                       Bernadette Carroll
                       Clare Constant
                       Emma Lee
                       Liz Lockwood

PEARSON
Longman

Contents
Speaking and Listening

Reading

Writing

Language

The Language strand is all about exploring and analysing the English language, developing your skills in investigating spoken and written English and exploring how it is used in different contexts, times and places. Developing your skills in the Language objectives will help you to improve your speaking and listening, reading and writing skills, so the Language objectives are covered in a range of speaking and listening, reading and writing units as are shown in the tables below.

Language in Speaking and Listening units

10.1	Exploring language variation and development according to time, place, culture, society and technology	AF6
10.2	Commenting on language use	AF3

Language in Reading units

10.1	Exploring language variation and development according to time, place, culture, society and technology	AF7
10.2	Commenting on language use	AF5

Language in Writing units

10.1	Exploring language variation and development according to time, place, culture, society and technology	AF6
10.2	Commenting on language use	AF1 AF2 AF4 AF5 AF7

LEARNING OBJECTIVES ⭐

- Select the most appropriate way to structure your talk to suit your audience and purpose.
- Use appropriate techniques to communicate information effectively in formal presentations about complex ideas.
- Use voice, body language and other resources to engage listeners' attention.

Activate your learning

1 Working in pairs, take turns in role as a magician and member of the audience to perform the trick below. The magician must convince the audience that the pencil has magic properties. (Make sure you use a pencil that is circular rather than hexagonal.)

The 'magician' should use the notes below to guide them through the trick. Try to use your **voice, body language** and **eye contact** to engage your audience, and to distract their attention from how the trick is performed.

★ Welcome your guests. Explain in formal terms how pencils are made of wood and so can have mysterious properties. Use words such as 'friction', 'molecular', 'magnetism'.

★ Lay the pencil on the table and start to rub a line from the pencil towards your side of the table. Ask members of the audience if they notice anything unusual. (They won't yet ...)

★ Explain that you are going to try the other direction and start to rub the table in a line from the pencil towards the audience's side of the table. Pay particular attention to the area close to the pencil.

★ Again, ask the audience if they notice anything unusual. As you do, blow the pencil ever so slightly so you don't see it move.

★ Rub the table close to the pencil in the direction of the audience. Look at the audience and blow the pencil towards them.

★ Explain how the 'static charge' cannot always be guaranteed and thank the audience.

2   When you have both had a go at performing the trick, discuss the following questions:

- How did the way the performance was organised help to hold the audience's attention?

- How did you use particular words and phrases to make the trick dramatic?

- Did you manage to distract your audience when necessary by using your voice, eye contact and body language?

3   Act out the performance of another magic trick. This might be one that you know, or you could make one up. Mime any props you might need, such as a deck of cards, but practise the speaking skills you have just used.

Assess to Progress

How good are you at organising the structure of your talk to keep an audience interested? Do you know how to use appropriate language to suit different situations and how to use your voice and body language to engage a listener's attention? For each skill tick the box under the description that you think best matches your current skill level.

I can ...	Easily	Sometimes	Not very often
structure talk to keep my audience interested. *Did you make the opening of the trick dramatic, build tension in the middle and surprise your audience at the end?*			
alter my talk to different situations. *Did you use formal language throughout and use scientific language to describe the magic properties of wood?*			
use voice, gesture and body language for effect. *Did you change the volume of your voice and use careful movements to direct the audience towards you and away from you when you needed to?*			

Build your skills

In this unit you are going to develop your skills in engaging the interest of your listeners when you speak and keeping their attention. The following text is an extract from a speech made by David Milliband MP about the challenge of saving the environment and tackling climate change. He opens with a reference to a crisis in London when the raw sewage in the Thames led to an overpowering smell.

1   Read the speech and then work with a his talk and how he could use voice, body language and other techniques to engage his audience's attention.

> a) How do you think this phrase was said?

> b) How does this immediately engage the audience?

In the summer of 1858, the House of Commons fell victim to what became known as the Great Stink. As the *Times* wrote at the time, 'Parliament was all but compelled to legislate upon the great London nuisance by the force of sheer stench.' The response was remarkably swift. Just 18 days after the chamber of the House of Commons had to be evacuated due to the stench of effluent in the Thames, a Bill was passed. The great engineer, Sir Joseph Bazalgette, was asked to draw up a massive new sewer scheme; and his project was responsible for successfully banishing cholera from the capital and serves London to this day.

> c) How might this image support the speaker in engaging the audience?

THE "SILENT HIGHWAY"-MAN

Today, I want to discuss how we can deal with today's Great Stink, climate change, and how we can mobilise the same combination of political will and practical innovation to address it. Today's Great Stink will not be solved by a single engineer, or a bill drawn up in 18 days. Furthermore, if we wait until the problem is at crisis point, it will be too late to put right.

> d) How do you think David Milliband might use his voice to deliver these lines?

My argument is this.

- The challenge of climate change is bigger, more immediate and will result in more human suffering than most people realise.

- The practical solutions, however, are increasingly available and cost effective, from advances in energy efficiency to renewable fuels for electricity, heat and transport.

- The challenge is for politics and policy to fundamentally change the way we live and work, pricing into our decisions, for the first time, the costs of climate change.

The idea that has captured the scale of the challenge and the interdependence of our action is what the WWF called One Planet living. The idea is simple: if everyone in the world were to consume natural resources and generate carbon dioxide at the rate we do in the UK, we'd need three planets to support us. We are depleting our natural resources at a far faster rate than we are replenishing them. We need instead to move towards a one-planet economy and one-planet living – where there is balance between what we give and what we take. This means deep reductions in CO_2 and other greenhouse gas emissions to a level the planet can sustain. It means a different way of living, working and travelling.

> e How does this section make the complex issue really clear for the audience?

> f How does this keep the audience interested?

> g How does this try to motivate the listeners to change their behaviour?

GLOSSARY

legislate – make laws
effluent – sewage put into a river
cholera – a dangerous infectious disease
depleting – reducing
interdependence – depending on each other

2 Discuss in a group whether you think the speech was effective at keeping your interest and attention. Discuss these questions:

- How was the talk structured to keep the audience's attention? Did it start well? Did it change in the middle? Did it have the right ending? What linked the two sections?

- What effect did the language David Milliband used have on his listeners? Pick out any parts of the speech that you think made his audience feel surprised or shocked or hopeful.

- How might the speaker have used his voice or body language at certain points to grab his audience's attention?

3 How could you use these and other images to support the speech? Discuss with a partner where you could most effectively include them.

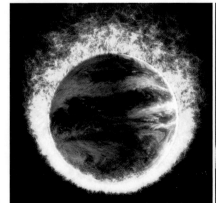

Reinforce your skills

Working in pairs, you are going to use your new skills to make a presentation about how polar bears are suffering due to the effects of global warming.

1 a) Read the three texts below and pick out any information that will be useful in your presentation.

   b) Decide which image best represents the information in each of the texts.

1

Slimmer than normal polar bears are a sign that the animals are having trouble obtaining enough food – a problem the WWF says is linked to global warming.
As early as 1999, Canadian researchers noticed that polar bears were having trouble finding enough seals to eat due to the break-up of sea ice earlier in the year. The scientists from the Canadian Wildlife Service found that weight for both male and female polar bears was declining, and female bears were having fewer cubs.

2

Global warming sees polar bears stranded on melting ice.
In Hudson Bay, where the ice melts completely in summer, scientists have noted that it is now happening three weeks earlier than normal. This is having a catastrophic effect on the bears, which hunt seals over the winter and spring before coming ashore, where they rely on their build-up of body fat to survive – and feed their cubs.

3

Since 1979, the size of the summer polar ice cap has shrunk more than 20 percent.
The polar ice cap as a whole is shrinking. Images from NASA satellites show that the area of permanent ice cover is contracting at a rate of 9 per cent each decade. If this trend continues, summers in the Arctic could become ice-free by the end of the century.

Polar ice cap: 1979

Polar ice cap: 1999

2 Work in pairs to plan your speech. Think of a title to grab your audience's attention and use the images to help you organise the information into sections. Think about:

- how you could start your talk – what information could you use to grab and keep your audience's attention?

- how you could use language for dramatic effect – what words could you use to show how serious the polar bears' situation is?

- how you could use your voice and body language – which points do you want to emphasise?

- how you are going to end your talk – what is the key message you want your audience to take away?

Support

You could structure your speech in three parts:

- Try to grab the audience's attention by showing the beauty of the polar bears.
- Use statistics and images to highlight how serious the issue is.
- Make your audience feel they can make a difference and save the polar bears.

When you practise your speech, remember to look directly at the audience, don't speak too quickly and pause for effect at key points. Try to vary the volume of your voice and give emphasis to key words and phrases.

Stretch

Think about how you could develop your speech to make it even more engaging for your listeners. Polar bears are not the only victims of global warming. Research additional material for your speech about the impact on other animals. **Remember to:**

- Try to use questioning techniques: ask your audience to think about the impact on them,

  e.g. *Will future generations have the chance to ...*
- Use body language, carefully timed pauses and images to provide impact.

Extend your skills

A powerful speech can live on long after the event. This speech was given by the civil rights leader Martin Luther King in 1963 when he believed that the biggest problem facing the United States was the fact that black people were not treated as equals. As you read the speech, look at how he used carefully chosen techniques, known as **rhetorical devices**, to influence and persuade his audience.

> He uses formal language to set a serious tone.

> He uses similes to create powerful images.

> Use of repetition for emphasis.

> Use of metaphor to make dramatic comparisons.

> Use of emotive language to engage the audience.

> Use of pronoun to bring people together.

Five score years ago, a great American, in whose symbolic shadow we stand today, signed the Emancipation Proclamation. This momentous decree came as a great beacon light of hope to millions of Negro slaves who had been seared in the flames of withering injustice. It came as a joyous daybreak to end the long night of their captivity.

But one hundred years later, the Negro still is not free. One hundred years later, the life of the Negro is still sadly crippled by the manacles of segregation and the chains of discrimination. One hundred years later, the Negro lives on a lonely island of poverty in the midst of a vast ocean of material prosperity. One hundred years later, the Negro is still languishing in the corners of American society and finds himself an exile in his own land. So we have come here today to dramatise a shameful condition.

GLOSSARY

five score years – a century

manacles – shackles or handcuffs

segregation – the separation or isolation of a race or ethnic group

1 Working in pairs, copy and complete the table below to help you explore how Martin Luther King engaged his listeners in this powerful speech.

How do you think the opening grabbed his listeners' attention?	What kind of language effects did the speaker use?	How do you think the speaker used his voice and body language to influence his listeners?

2 Practise reading the speech to your partner. Think about how you can use your voice, gestures and body language to emphasise the rhetorical devices used and have a powerful effect on your listener.

Apply your learning

Over 100 years ago, Alexander Graham Bell, the inventor of the telephone, announced, 'One day every major city in America will have a telephone.' Nowadays, every single person seems to have a telephone! Predicting the future is a tricky business, especially when technology is changing so quickly.

Task How do you think the world will have changed in 50 years' time? Prepare a formal presentation to give to the rest of the class explaining your ideas. Think about how current technology, such as mobile phones and computers, might have changed, what new inventions we might be using and what effect these will have on the way we live our lives.

As you prepare your presentation, remember to:

- use a clear structure to make your ideas clear to your audience

- use different techniques and rhetorical devices to persuade your listeners that your view of the future might come true

- use your voice and body language to engage your listeners.

Assess to Progress

How good are you now at structuring your talk to keep an audience interested? Can you use appropriate language to suit different situations and use your voice and body language to engage listeners? Look back at the table you completed on page 3. Think about the presentation you have just given, then for each skill tick the box under the description that you now think best matches your skill level.

Your headteacher wants you to give a speech in assembly persuading pupils and teachers to recycle more and save energy. Work in groups to discuss the different things people could do.

Then prepare and present your speech persuading pupils and teachers to act in environmentally friendly ways.

LEARNING OBJECTIVES

- Pick out significant details from what a speaker says and make contributions that help to develop the speaker's ideas.
- Analyse the different techniques that speakers use and identify the ways they could make improvements to communicate more effectively.
- Interpret and make inferences from what a speaker says in different speaking situations.

Activate your learning

Alan Franks is a well-known journalist and interviewer for the *Times* newspaper. He has made the following points about how to interview celebrities successfully.

Go along with what they want to talk about. For a little while anyway.

Try to meet them on their home territory.

Treat them naturally.

Have the next question in your head, ready to go. And the one after that.

Pray: it's a weird, unguessable business. You don't know what sort of mood they're going to be in.

Make sure your tape recorder is running.

Expect them to be different from what you'd expected.

Get plenty of stuff in the can before you ask the tricky questions.

Ask the questions which you feel others would most want to ask.

Don't judge them on what you've heard or read about them; judge them for yourself.

1   Working in a group of four, spend five minutes discussing these points and deciding which is the most important, which is the least important and then rank order the rest.

One person in the group should act as the note-taker, recording the main points of what has been said and by whom. If you are note-taker, note down key points and add initials by the side to show who said what.

2   a)   At the end of the discussion, the note-taker should tell the speakers what ideas they gave and their reasons.

b)   The speakers should then discuss how accurate they think the record of the discussion is. Do you think you said more? Did the note-taker miss any important points that you made?

Assess to Progress

How good are you at listening and responding to what somebody says? Rate yourself for each of the following skills by deciding where you would place yourself on the scale below. You will need to justify your decisions, so try to think of examples that support your choice.

1		3	4	5	6	7

I find this difficult.   I'm getting there.   I'm good at this.

- I can recognise significant details from what a speaker says and make contributions that develop their ideas in different ways.

  Self-check: You can identify what the important points are in what people say and you ask questions and make suggestions that build on what others say.

- I can analyse the effect of different techniques and strategies that a speaker uses and identify areas for improvement.

  Self-check: You recognise when a speaker is using a technique such as asking rhetorical questions to get the audience to listen and think. You can think of ways in which a speaker could improve their talk.

- I can interpret and make inferences from speech in a variety of contexts.

  Self-check: You can spot a speaker's point of view and how they feel from what they say.

Build your skills

You are going to watch part of an episode of *Top Gear*, where Jeremy Clarkson is speaking to the comedian Harry Enfield about his views on cars. In this clip, Jeremy Clarkson introduces his guest and shows what he thinks about the car he drives. Watch the clip, then follow the skill steps to explore what you can find out from what he says and how he says it.

Step 1   Identify different techniques and analyse their effect

1   a)   What techniques does Jeremy Clarkson use to share his views? Working with a partner, watch the clip again and find instances where he:

   ● uses examples to support his ideas

   ● pauses for effect

   ● says one thing but means another

   ● uses lists of three

   ● uses repetition

   ● leaves the main information until last to interest the listener.

   b)   With your partner, copy and complete the table below, picking out more examples of the techniques Jeremy Clarkson uses and explaining what effect you think these have.

Technique	Example	Why he uses it
Pause for effect	'Ladies and Gentlemen … Harry Enfield!'	The pause makes the build-up to the guest more dramatic.
Repetition	'big time … big-time'	To make the audience think Harry is a 'big-time' star and also to make his choice of car seem more ridiculous.

Step 2 Infer and interpret what a speaker means

When listening to a speaker you can sometimes **infer** (work out) what their opinion is, even when they do not give it directly.

1   Working with a partner, decide whether the following statements about Jeremy Clarkson's opinions are true or false. Find evidence to support your decisions.

A He expects actors or comedians to buy expensive, fast cars.	D The Vauxhall Cavalier convertible is a terrible car.
B All actors or comedians have expensive, fast cars.	E Harry Enfield bought the car to make people laugh.
C Norman Wisdom has an expensive, fast car.	F He thinks Harry Enfield is ridiculous.

2   We can infer that Jeremy Clarkson believes Harry Enfield's choice of car is ridiculous, even though he does not say so. Watch the interview, and pick out the clues that help you to **deduce** this, e.g. he says 'what **possessed** you to buy one'.

3   Look back at the list of techniques on page 12. What techniques does Harry Enfield use when he speaks? Continue your table, picking out examples of the techniques he uses.

4   Now watch the interview again and focus on what Jeremy Clarkson says. Do you think he is responding well to what Harry Enfield has said? What advice could you give him to improve his interviewing skills?

Reinforce your skills

You are now going to practise your own interviewing technique. Your school librarian has arranged for the author, William Nicholson, to give a talk to pupils and then answer questions from the audience.

You have been asked to devise some questions to put to the author. Use the web page below to help you to prepare.

WILLIAM NICOHLSON **BIOGRAPHY**

HOME - Q & A - FANTASY BOOKS - NOVELS -FILMS & PLAYS -BIOGRAPHY - AGENTS

William Nicholson was born in 1948 and brought up in England. After university, he joined the BBC as a documentary film maker. He started writing screenplays whilst working for the BBC and he won many awards for his television screenplays. He also wrote film screenplays and co-wrote *Gladiator* starring Russell Crowe. As a film screenplay writer, he has received two Oscar nominations. He's also written stage plays. Nicholson wrote a trilogy for older children, starting with *The Wind Singer*, continued in *Slaves of the Mastery* and concluded with *Firesong*. His second sequence of books for older children is entitled *The Noble Warriors*. He has also written two books for adults.

---

1   Work in pairs to prepare five questions that you would like to ask William Nicholson about his second trilogy of books, *The Noble Warriors*. Think of questions that will encourage him to give interesting answers and detail he may not cover in his talk.

2   Now read what William Nicholson said in his talk. Which of your prepared questions does he answer?

'You know, when I decided to write a second trilogy ... because I've already written a trilogy ... fantasy books ... I wanted to do the most important thing that I knew how to do ... because this takes a lot of my life, you know, three books ... five years, probably, of my life ... so I wasn't going to mess about. I wasn't going to do something that I didn't really care about, I was going to do the thing I cared most about, so I thought to myself, "I want this to be about characters that I love, I want it to be stories that I'm compelled by, and I want it to be in a world and with a background to it that actually means something important" ... so that's quite a ... quite a demand ... So that's how it began ... and so then I sat down and I said, "What really turns me on most?" and the answer was the search for God. Now that may seem strange, but actually, I'm not sure about God ... at all ... and I thought ... I want to go on this search with my characters.'

3 Look at the following four questions. Rank them in order of relevance and usefulness having heard the initial speech.

What made you start writing your second trilogy?
What is there about fantasy stories that interests you the most?
Did you get to meet Russell Crowe on the set of *Gladiator*?
Were you cross that you didn't win an Oscar?

4 Which would be the best question to ask next? Which question would show you had listened to what William Nicholson had already said? Write three more questions that you would ask him next.

> ## Support
>
> Think about how you can ask questions to help you clarify what a speaker means or develop their ideas:
> • When you said ... did you mean ...?
> • How did you ...?

Extend your skills

When you listen to somebody speak, it is important to be able to respond to what they say. To do this, you need to identify their most important points and encourage the speaker to develop these further. You can do this by supporting what they say or challenging their ideas.

The following text is a sketch from a TV comedy show, where three characters are discussing buying a new car. What do you notice about Dave's response when someone challenges his view?

FRIEND 1	I was thinking of getting one of those new C-Class Mercedes.
DAVE	No ... you don't want to get yourself one of them. They're rubbish! You wanna get yourself a jeep ... one of them Cherokee Jeeps. Brilliant family car. Get six kids and a dog in the back of one of those, no trouble.
FRIEND 2	They aren't that big, Dave.
DAVE	No, they're not really when you get a look at them, no.

1 What would you say to the first man to get him to talk about why he is thinking of buying a C-Class Mercedes?

2 Work with a partner to devise a list of rules to follow to help you to develop a speaker's ideas.

3 Look at the rules Ben suggests below. Identify the important points and then explain how you could respond to Ben to get him to develop these ideas.

You should let people talk about what they want to because it would get them to open up to you and relax, ... they might tell you something by accident if they trust you ... but you shouldn't just let them talk, because then they might not tell you the really interesting things you want to know.

Stretch

Think about how you could give constructive feedback to Ben to help him to express his ideas more clearly. Try to explain what he does well and which skills he needs to improve.

Apply your learning

Task You are going to role-play a phone-in on a local radio programme for a ten-minute slot entitled *If I Ruled the World*. Working with a partner, one of you will play a radio presenter and the other will play the part of somebody who has phoned in to the station. Follow the steps below as you role-play the phone-in interview.

1 If you are playing the phone-in guest, pass a brief note to your partner, giving some information about what you will be talking about.

2 If you are the radio presenter, make some brief notes about your views on what the phone-in caller will be talking about and list three or four questions you could ask.

3 Now perform your radio interview role play. Then swap roles so that you both have a chance to play the caller and the interviewer.

Assess to Progress

How good are you now at listening and responding to what somebody says? Look back at the ratings you gave yourself on page 11. Now rate yourself again for each of the skills below by deciding which number on the scale best shows your skill level. Pick out examples that show your skill level from the task you have just completed.

| 1 | 2 | 3 | 4 | 5 | 6 | 7 |

I find this difficult.   I'm getting there.   I'm good at this.

- I can recognise significant details from what a speaker says and make contributions that develop their ideas in different ways.
- I can analyse the effect of different techniques and strategies that a speaker uses and identify areas for improvement.
- I can interpret and make inferences from speech in a variety of contexts.

SKILLs FOR LIFE

Your local council is holding a meeting to allow teenagers to comment on plans for improving facilities in your area. Working in a group of four, discuss which of the following proposals you think would be the best idea. You should each choose one proposal to talk about so that each idea gets a fair hearing.

To improve the local all-weather pitch by building a pavilion that can be used as a shelter. This will include changing rooms and showers.	To improve after-school activities in the local area by giving four after-school clubs money for a suite of ten computers.
To improve the local skateboard park by building three more ramps and create a wall for budding graffiti artists to practise and display their artwork.	To give all teenagers a pass that allows them to go swimming one night a week after school at the local swimming baths.

Remember to listen carefully to the points other members of your group make and respond to these to help develop their ideas.

Progress in ... Developing speaking skills in formal and informal situations

LEARNING OBJECTIVES

- Understand how to structure what you say clearly and effectively according to your purpose and audience.
- Use spoken standard English, adapting the level of formality to suit different situations.
- Use what you know about speaking for different reasons and audiences and choosing your style and vocabulary appropriately.

Activate your learning

Read the following newspaper report.

Painful times for plucky pupil

Plucky teenager Harry Smith is today recovering in hospital after being knocked down at a pedestrian crossing on his way to school on Wednesday.

Although Harry has broken his leg and has several broken ribs, he is remaining cheerful and is set to make a full recovery. Harry maintains that the green lights were in his favour and that the car which knocked him down went through a red light. The motorist is disputing this and says that it was Harry who crossed the road on a red light. Police are appealing for anyone who witnessed the accident to contact them.

1 a) Working in a group of four, take it in turns to create the role plays on the cards below. In each role play think about how you can adapt what you say to the situation you are in and the people you are speaking to.

You are two friends of Harry who were with him when the accident happened. When you get to school, you tell your mates all about it.

You are a passenger in the car which knocked Harry over. Give your account of the accident to the police officer.

You are a shopkeeper who saw the whole thing.
Tell the newspaper reporter your story.

You are the local radio DJ and are reporting the accident on air.

b) While each role play is taking place, the remaining members of the group should make notes about how formal each situation is and how language choices change according to who is being spoken to and why. Think about:

- what sort of vocabulary is being used
- what sort of sentence structure is being used
- whether anyone is using standard English
- whether you hear any examples of slang
- whether the choices are appropriate for the character.

2 Share your ideas about how formal or informal each role play situation was and explain whether the language choices each speaker made were appropriate and why.

Assess to Progress

How good do you think you are already at adapting what you say according to the situation you are in? Rate yourself for each of the following skills by deciding which number on the scale below best shows your skill level.

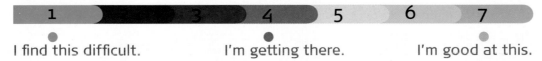

| 1 | 3 | 4 | 5 | 6 | 7 |

I find this difficult.   I'm getting there.   I'm good at this.

- I understand why I need to vary what I say according to my purpose and audience.

  Self-check: If you were asked to give a talk or take part in an interview, would you know that you need to make what you say appropriate for the situation?

- I understand what standard English is and can vary the formality of what I say.

  Self-check: If you had to give a statement about an accident you had witnessed, would you be able to make your account of it different depending on whether you were talking to your headteacher or to your friends?

- I can use what I know about speaking for different reasons and audiences and choose my style and vocabulary appropriately.

  Self-check: Can you decide on and use the techniques that are appropriate to the speaking situation you are in, e.g. a job interview?

Build your skills

When you speak, it is important to choose a level of **formality** that is appropriate to the situation. Below is a transcript of an interview with a student who wants to take a travel and tourism course at his local college. The interviewer is a teacher who wants to get a full picture of the applicants' qualities.

1 Before you look at the transcript, discuss with a partner:

- how formal you might expect this situation to be

- how you would expect the student to make a good impression on the teacher

- what sorts of things the teacher might want to find out.

2 Working in pairs, read the transcript aloud. One of you should take the part of Dan Cole, the interviewer, and the other of Elliot Sellar, the student being interviewed.

[knock on the door]

Dan: *Please come in ... Hi, I'm Dan Cole.*

Elliot: *I'm Elliot Sellar.*

Dan: *So, I'm the course leader for the travel and tourism part of the college. Have you been here before? Are you familiar with the place?*

Elliot: *Yeah ... erm ... my team's played against this college before...yeah.*

Dan: *What, your football team?*

Elliot: *Yeah ... football ... sorry.*

Dan: *So how did you get on?*

Elliot: *We smashed 'em!*

Dan: *[Laughs] Oh really! I thought we had quite a good team!*

Elliot: *No ... they're all right, but ... erm ... like, we've been together for a long time.*
[Mobile phone rings] Sorry ... Hello? Hello mate! How ya doin'? No ... listen ... you caught me at a bit of an odd ... an awkward time ... I'll call you in about ... 20 minutes? Awright, cool mate ... Cheers! Bye ... Sorry about that.

Dan: *OK. Could you ensure it's turned off, just to make sure ...*

Elliot: *Yeah ...*

Language

3 With your partner, look at the speaking checklist below and discuss each point in turn, assessing how well Elliot achieves these points.

Speaking checklist

- **Clarity** — Does he make himself clear?
- **Audience** — Has he taken the needs of his listener into account?
- **Purpose** — Is the purpose clear?
- **Style** — Do you think he has chosen the right sort of vocabulary and sentence structure for his audience and purpose?
- **Structure** — Is there a clear beginning, development and conclusion to what he says?
- **Formality** — Has he chosen the right level of formality? Does he use standard English?
- **Expression** — Does he adapt his tone of voice or vary the pace at which he speaks to interest his listener and emphasise the points he wants to make?
- **Body language** — Does he use appropriate gestures and facial expressions to engage his listener? Does he maintain eye contact?

4 Now act out this alternative role play and with reference to the checklist discuss how it is different from the first one.

[knock on the door]

Dan: *Hello, come in, please come in. Hi, I'm Dan Cole.*

Elliot: *Hi, I'm Elliot Sellar.*

Dan: *Take a seat. So … I see from your CV you're pretty keen on football.*

Elliot: *Yeah … erm … I play for Leightonstone Football Club, which is local to me.*

Dan: *And it says you're captain.*

Elliot: *Yeah … and as well as being captain of the team on the field, I do a lot of the off-field activities. I play kind of like the role of an assistant manager and I manage a lot of the schedules and where we play and who we play against.*

Dan: *So what's the furthest you've been on one of these trips?*

Elliot: *Er … we went to Le Touquet not too long ago, in France, and we really enjoyed ourselves. All the boys were all on the coach and it was good fun, really good fun. It was a knockout tournament and we got knocked out in the fifth round, so it wasn't too bad.*

Language

Reinforce your skills

Working with your partner, read out the following extract from one of Jamie Oliver's podcasts about cooking Barbeque chicken thighs.

OK. I'm gonna do you some chicken legs. Chicken thighs, always a problem, people cookin' them, look lovely, eat into them, raw in the middle near the bone, nightmare. You've either got to eat 'em, er, an' get them nice and golden and take 'em to the core part of the barbecue, an' it takes about half an hour, 35 minutes to get them good, so they just fall apart, off the bone. If they fall off the bone, you're laughing. If you've got to tug 'em, you know it's not cooked yet.

I wanna show you something that's another cheat – it's a way of getting mega flavour into your chicken. I've got some tin foil, right, and I just … ahh!!! … oohh!!! *[the foil is hot on the barbecue]* Let me just grab that. I've got some tin foil and two layers of tin foil. Have a look in here. I've cooked this in the barbie with the lid down, or you could do it in an oven at about 180 centigrade or 350 fahrenheit. Look. Chicken thighs, right? I've put a whole load of garlic, skin on and everything in there, come back to that, half a lemon in there, come back to that, right, and a bit of rosemary. OK. It's already got seasoning on it, so at this point in the story, this chicken is absolutely cooked. It's going straight onto the barbecue and we're going to get that golden.

1   Who do you think is the audience for Jamie Oliver's podcast? How might that affect the type of language he uses and the level of formality he chooses?

2   a)   Try changing the podcast so that he gives all his instructions in standard English.

   b)   Compare the changes you have made with another pair's. Discuss what effect this new podcast would have on the audience. What do you think has been lost and what has been gained?

> ### Stretch
> In the style of Jamie Oliver, give instructions on *How to Make a Cup of Tea* for his next video podcast.

Extend your skills

In this speech, the speaker is trying to persuade his audience to agree with his way of thinking. You would usually expect to hear someone speaking like this in more formal situations, but because such a light-hearted topic is being spoken about in such a serious way this makes the speech humorous.

1   Working in pairs, read the speech below and decide where you might hear somebody speaking in this way.

Ban the Biscuit

Chocolate biscuit. Chocolate. Biscuit.

And I still remember where I was when I first heard those words, how it made me feel. I was eight years old. It was Christmas and my grandfather just came out with it. 'Do you want a chocolate biscuit?' A chocolate biscuit. Two things that to my eight-year-old mind were as close to heaven as I could imagine in one: the crunchy, oatmeal buttery-ness of a biscuit actually combined with the creamy, sweet yummy-ness of chocolate. And how did I feel when I bit into this delicious first chocolate digestive, you ask? Well, I felt privileged. I felt renewed. I felt special. And on that day I knew my life would never be the same again.

I didn't know I had a problem, until a kindly Geography master told me what I'm going to tell you now: life is about more than biscuits! Certainly, they tasted good. Of course, they hadn't made me ill. Naturally, I thought I could handle them. But let me tell you, I couldn't. No one can.

Many people say, 'Ah, I've eaten my fill of chocolate biscuits, and I'm fine!' Well, I'm here to tell you, you're not fine! You're very far from being fine! Just imagine, for the moment, how different your life would be if you hadn't spent so much of it stuffing down those delicious discs of danger.

Now, on the one hand, chocolate biscuits are a delicious, nutritious, snack food. On the other, they are a dangerous parasite gnawing at the very heart, the very fabric of society. And we know what we do with parasites, don't we?! We cut them out!

I want, I demand that all production, distribution, consumption of chocolate biscuits ends now. Not tomorrow, not next week, not next month, but now and for ever! My friends, until we face this challenge, and face it together, this country, this nation, will continue to crumble … My friends, it is time for everyone, all of us to break away from those tempting treats, rise up against them and in one clear voice, proclaim,

'Ban the biscuit! Ban the biscuit!! BAN THE BISCUIT!!!'

2 This speaker uses a number of **rhetorical devices** to engage the audience and emphasise his message. Working with your partner, see how many examples of the following techniques you can find in the speech:

- **Rhetorical questions** — where the speaker does not really expect an answer.

- **Emotive language** — encouraging a listener to imagine strong emotions, e.g. pleasure, fear.

- **Parallel structures** — structuring sentences to achieve some sort of balance, e.g. 'To show kindness is praiseworthy; to show hatred is evil.'

- **Sound patterns** — such as **alliteration** (repeating sounds at the beginning of words, e.g. 'All advertisers are alike') or **assonance** (repeating sounds within words, e.g. 'Try to light the fire.')

- **Contrasts** — e.g. 'Being cruel to be kind.'

- **Description** and **imagery** — using **metaphor**, **simile** and **personification**.

- **Rule of three** — e.g. 'Is this fair, is it right, is it just?'

- **Repetition** — where key words and phrases are repeated.

- **Hyperbole** — using exaggeration for effect, e.g. 'The whole world holds its breath.'

- **Anecdote** — a short and interesting story taken from the speaker's own experience.

Apply your learning

Task You have been invited to give a pupil's view on what changes could be made to the school canteen to the school governors, who want to encourage more pupils to use the facility. Prepare a formal two-minute speech in which you set out to persuade the governors of your point of view.

Before you make your speech, plan what you could cover in your talk. You might want to cover the following topics:

- how menus could be made tastier or move interesting
- possible events or theme days
- how to improve the surroundings and service.

Think about how you can choose the style and vocabulary appropriate to your purpose and audience. **Remember to:**

- use standard English and choose the right level of formality
- use the different rhetorical techniques you have explored
- think about the way you can engage and maintain the interest and attention of your audience.

Assess to Progress

How good do you think you are now at adapting what you say according to the situation you are in? Look back at the ratings you gave on page 19. Now rate yourself again for each of the skills by deciding which number on the scale best shows your skill level. Pick out examples that show your skill level from the task you have just completed.

SKILLS FOR LIFE

You have been asked to introduce a guest speaker who is going to address your school about the importance of healthy eating. Using the information below, prepare and present an introduction that will encourage the audience to listen carefully to what the speaker has to say.

- The number of school children who are obese has doubled in ten years.
- Nearly one quarter of adults are obese.
- Children with obese parents are twice as likely to become obese.
- Children who are obese in their early teens are twice as likely to die by the age of 50.
- Eating an unbalanced diet can lead to serious health problems.

In your introduction you should: explain who the speaker is and what they will be talking about and; make sure the audience realise why this is an important topic.

Your introduction should be no more than one minute long.

LEARNING OBJECTIVES ⭐

- Understand how to take different roles in discussion.
- Make a sustained contribution in discussion, illustrating and explaining your ideas.
- Listen carefully, asking pertinent questions and making suggestions in order to solve problems and test ideas.

Activate your learning

Do you know how to take on different roles in a group to make sure that your discussion is successful? Look at the following roles that people take in group discussions.

The main speaker — says the most and leads the discussion
The agreer — agrees with everything everyone else says, adding 'yeah' or 'uh-huh' to show he or she is listening
The builder — takes what someone else has said and adds to it, developing and agreeing with the ideas put forward
The negative — challenges everything that is said, dismissing it and questioning whether it would work or not
The questioner — doesn't often add anything directly or make statements, but asks other people questions to prompt them
The thinker — sits back and listens for a long time and then says something that takes the discussion forward quickly
The springboard — says something completely unrelated to anything that has been said before which really takes the discussion forward
The chairperson — does not say very much but makes people in the group feel welcome and able to contribute
The time-keeper — acts as task manager to keep people focused and encourage them to move on

1　Working in a group of four, discuss the nine roles described on the previous page. Three of you should discuss the statements and a fourth group member should observe and take notes.

a) First of all, decide which three types of individual from those listed are most helpful in group discussions. You have three minutes to decide.

b) Now swap roles, with the observer taking part in the discussions, and the person the observer says has spoken the most taking the role of the observer. Decide which three types of individual would be least helpful in group work. You have three minutes to decide.

c) Finally, the pupils who have acted as observers should explain what types of role they have seen in the group discussions, giving examples of things that have been said.

Assess to Progress

How well can you contribute to group discussions already? Use what you have learnt about yourself while taking part in the previous discussion as well as your experiences of other group work to help you rank yourself for each of the skills below.

1	2	3	4	5	6	7

I find this difficult.　　　　I'm getting there.　　　　I'm good at this.

● I know how to take a variety of roles in discussion.

 Self-check: Do you know that sometimes it is necessary to change roles and adopt a different approach to move the discussion forward?

● I make sustained contributions in discussion and know how to illustrate and explain my ideas.

 Self-check: Do you give examples or explain your ideas without members of your group asking you to do so?

● I can listen carefully, asking pertinent questions and making suggestions in order to solve problems and test ideas.

 Self-check: Do you understand how important it is to ask questions to challenge people and know how to encourage other people to contribute?

Build your skills

Contributing and sustaining the creative flow of ideas in a discussion are essential skills for group interaction. Explore how you can do this by working through the skill steps below.

Step 1 Generate ideas

Some people struggle to contribute to group discussion because they do not have enough ideas. Here, Alex is taking part in a discussion about the benefits of mobile phones. The diagram below shows his thoughts.

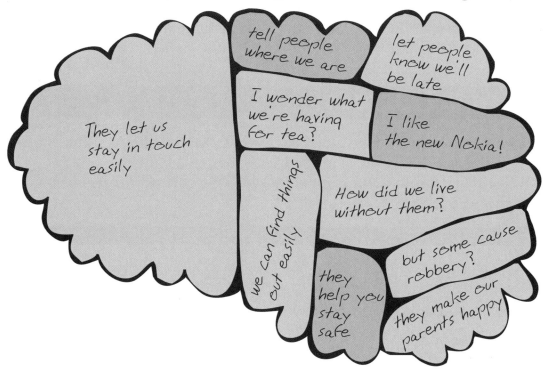

When preparing for a discussion you should brainstorm as many ideas as you can about the topic, then ask yourself the following questions:

- Are all of my thoughts relevant? e.g. 'I like the new Nokia' isn't really connected to the benefits of mobile phones.

- Can I expand on any idea by adding examples to it? e.g. If I talk about how they make our parents happy, I can explain how my mum feels better if she knows where I am.

- Have I got any ideas I need to explain? e.g. Would need to explain how mobile phones keep you safe because it's not obvious.

1 a) Create a diagram of your own thoughts and ideas about this topic. Use whatever kind of format you feel is appropriate, e.g. a list or a spider diagram.

   b) Compare your ideas with a partner's. Which ideas do you think you would use in the discussion?

Step 2 Develop your contributions

You can develop and sustain your ideas when contributing to a group discussion by giving examples or explaining in more detail what you mean.

Adding an example might support the point you are trying to make. An example could be an anecdote (a short story describing something that happened to you), a piece of evidence or even some statistics.

1   In the following transcript Alex gives an example to support his idea. Look back at your own ideas and think about which ones you could add to by giving examples.

> Alex: *I think mobile phones are a good thing because they keep your parents happy. My mum doesn't worry as much when she knows she can get hold of me at any time she likes ... she's a bit of a worrier! The other Saturday, she was reading a newspaper and read a story about a boy who'd fallen in a lake, so she rang me just to ask me where I was and make sure I wasn't hanging around any lakes! It's a good thing because if she hadn't been able to get in touch with me, she'd be worried sick by the time I got home!*

Explaining and expanding your ideas so that they are clear is also useful in group discussion.

2   a)   Look at how Alex does this in the transcript below. Working with a partner, identify how Alex explains his idea.

   b)   Look back at your own ideas and think about which ones you could explain in a similar way.

> Alex: *Mobile phones are a benefit because we can use them to find things out easily, even if we're not at home or at a computer. You can send a text to someone to find out what your homework is, and even if they're having their tea or doing something else, they'll still text you back if they know. If you'd phoned their house line, they might not be at home or they might be doing something with their family, so you might be interrupting them or you might not find out.*

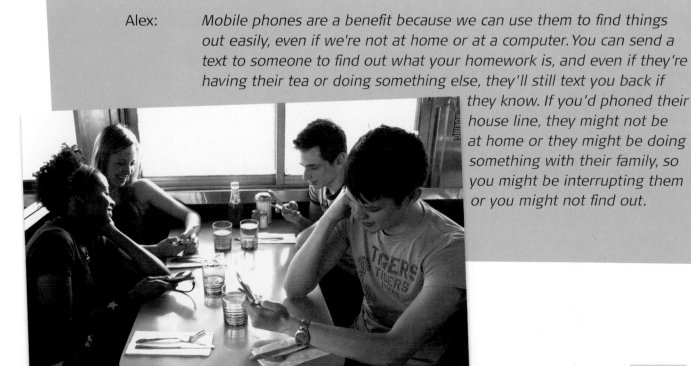

Another way to develop your contributions is by **hypothesising** or **speculating**. This means putting forward ideas or considering consequences that you have no evidence for.

3 Can you identify the speculative language Alex uses here? Think about how you could use this language to develop your own ideas.

> Alex: *Mobile phones must be a benefit because I can't imagine how we lived without them. We'd probably have got into loads of trouble for being late and not telling our mum we were going to be late, or we might have come back late and got grounded. I think there would have been more arguments between mums and their children!*

Reinforce your skills

It is also important to be able to contribute to a discussion in a way that shows you can listen and respond to others' ideas. Here, Beverley, Carol and Paul are discussing travelling by plane.

Beverley: *I got upgraded to business class last time we flew.*

Carol: *And what was that like?*

Beverley: *It was amazing because you get ... well, the best thing about business class is you get proper beds, so there's none of that business of falling asleep next to some snoring stranger that you get in economy.*

Carol: *That sounds great – how does that work though? How do they get the beds in?*

Beverley: *You're kind of staggered ... I can't really explain it.*

Paul: *Are they over-lapping? You don't lie there next to some stranger like two twin beds right next to each other?*

Beverley: *Yes, the beds are staggered and overlap, so you're kind of facing the other bed. You can draw a screen between you as well, so you don't wake up face to face with some stranger. Of course, it's alright if you're travelling with people you know, but if you are on your own, I'd feel quite weird waking up with a stranger!*

Carol: *So you'd rather wake up with your husband's feet in your face?*

Beverley: *No ...[laughs] it's not like that. There's a screen between you anyway. I suppose it could be quite odd if you were really travelling on business.*

Paul: *... like if you were flying to New York for work...*

Beverley: *Mmmm.*

Paul: *Of course, the other good thing about business class is that you can use the lounge at the airport. If you fly from Heathrow, you can even use the spa. It's a world away from flying economy. I look at the people flying economy and I'm sitting there, relaxed and chilled out.*

1 What techniques can you see Paul and Carol using when Beverley is speaking? Working with a partner, can you find examples of:

- asking relevant questions to help Beverley develop what she is saying?

- picking up on what Beverley has just said?

- giving her speculative ideas or reasons to help her explain?

- testing what is said and challenging Beverley?

- putting Beverley's ideas into their own words to show they understand?

- helping Beverley explain?

Support

Working in a group of three, read aloud the discussion between Carol, Beverley and Paul. Take it in turns to read out Carol and Paul's contributions. As you read, think about whether the contribution helps to promote or back up the idea that Beverley is presenting or whether it questions or opposes it.

Extend your skills

When somebody else is presenting their ideas, there are several ways you can help them to test or develop their thinking. Look at how you can use the following key words in group discussion.

- **Words and phrases that find solutions** — e.g. 'unless', 'except', 'although':

Sarah	*We couldn't live without mobile phones ...*
Mark	*Unless?*
Sarah	**Unless** *... we made lots of changes in our life.*

- **Words that help us speculate** — e.g. 'perhaps', 'probably', 'possibly', 'maybe':

  | Sarah | *We couldn't live without mobile phones ...* |
  | Mark | **Perhaps** *we could if we found alternatives.* |

- **Words and phrases that give examples** — e.g. 'for instance', 'for example', 'such as', 'you know when', 'it's like':

  | Sarah | *We couldn't live without mobile phones ...* |
  | Mark | **You know when** *you're a bit late and you need to let your mum know you'll be home late, then they're a real life-saver! They stop your mum worrying about you!* |

1 a) Working in a group of four, discuss what you think are the benefits of mobile phones. Look back at the ideas you generated on page 28 and use the techniques you have learnt to develop your contributions. Make sure that each member of the group has a chance to present their ideas, and think about how you can help to develop their contributions.

   b) Summarise the key points from your discussion and be ready to report these back to the rest of the class.

Stretch

In your group, take on the role of chairperson and think about how you can draw together ideas made by different members of the group to help move the discussion forward.

Apply your learning

You are now going to use the skills you have developed through the unit to help you to complete the task below.

Task Your headteacher is concerned that mobile phones are having a negative effect in school. He is worried about the way mobile phone calls are disrupting lessons, incidences of bullying by text message and thefts of mobiles from school bags. He wants to create a new school policy encouraging pupils to use their mobile phones responsibly.

Working in a group of four, discuss and devise a set of ten simple rules for pupils in your school that encourage them to use their phones appropriately, and explain why.

In your group discussion, you will need to show that you can:

- take a range of different roles, such as the chairperson who manages the discussion or the spokesperson who reports back.

- develop your contributions by adding examples, explanations, hypothesising and speculating.

- help others develop their contributions by probing what they say, asking questions and making suggestions.

Assess to Progress

How good are you now at contributing effectively to group discussions? Look back at your original ratings on page 27 and decide where you would now place yourself on the scale below. Use what you have learnt about yourself while taking part in the previous activity to support your decisions and explain your reasons to a partner.

1   2   3   4   5   6   7

I find this difficult.   I'm getting there.   I'm good at this.

- I know how to take a variety of roles in discussion.

- I make sustained contributions in discussion and know how to illustrate and explain my ideas.

- I can listen carefully, asking pertinent questions and making suggestions in order to solve problems and test ideas.

Now answer the following questions.

1   What have you learnt that you did not know or could not do before?

2   What was the hardest part of this unit?

The School Council has been asked to investigate the ways in which pupils can be rewarded for good behaviour or excellent performances whether in academic work or in school activities, such as team sports or drama. The following ideas have been suggested in a survey of pupils' opinions.

- Free tickets to a sports event, such as a Premiership football match.

- Free entry to the local sports centre for a month.

- Arranging a concert with a local band at the school.

Working in a group, discuss the suggestions and decide which would be the best way to reward pupils. You can also add and discuss your own suggestions.

When you have decided, prepare and make a presentation to the governors summarising what your group decided and giving the reasons for your decision. Think about the best way of presenting your recommendations and how you should speak.

Speaking and Listening AF5
Progress in ... Drama, role play and performance

- Use dramatic approaches to explore ideas, texts, issues and themes in structured ways.
- Use dramatic conventions and techniques to develop and sustain stories, roles and performances.
- Evaluate the impact and effectiveness of using different dramatic techniques.

Activate your learning

In this unit you are going to use different dramatic approaches to help you explore some of the ideas in the novel *No Angels* by Robert Swindells. It is about a teenage girl called Nikki who decides to run away from home to London as her mother's boyfriend, Ronnie, is trying to strike up an inappropriate relationship with her.

1   a) Working in a group, decide in what order you think the five events below occur.

   b) Discuss how you think the words would be spoken by the character or narrator.

A (Nikki) I've found this doorway up a narrow street called Barr Street. If I bend forward and look left I can see people passing on Oxford Street ... I don't half wish I had a sleeping bag.

B (Nikki in the squat) While the three of them chat I kneel at the hearth, feeding the fire with splinters and stirring the stew ... They're all really nice to me about the stew and the cleaning.

C (Nikki's mum) 'No, he did not, Nikki. You're dramatising, trying to drive a wedge between Ronnie and me because you've never liked him. Well it won't work, my girl, so you might as well ...'

D (Nikki lying in a hospital bed speaking to a police officer) 'One of the guys, I don't know his real name. He says Ronnie might try to put me out of the way so I can't give evidence.'

E (Nikki) I wake to the creak of the letter-flap, a small thud ... Demi! I choke. Wake up, the house is on fire ...

2 a) As a group, create a series of tableaux to tell Nikki's story. In each tableau the action of an event should be captured through the character's body language and expressions.

b) Groups should take it in turns to watch each other's performance and decide which tableau worked best. Think about:

- how well each person used body language and facial expression to show what their character was experiencing

- how well the group positioned the characters so that you could tell what the situation was and how they felt about it.

c) Choose one tableau and suggest ways in which it could be improved to better express part of the story.
e.g. The people on the street should look happy and relaxed. In contrast Nikki should curl up tight like she's shivering and frightened.

Assess to Progress

How confident are you already at using dramatic techniques such as tableaux, role play, mime and performance to explore ideas about a situation, character or issue? Rate yourself for each of the skills below and decide which number on the scale best shows your skill level as you think about the activities you have just done.

1	2	3	4	5	6	7

I find this difficult.   I'm getting there.   I'm good at this.

- I can use dramatic approaches such as tableaux to explore ideas and characters.

  Self-check: How much did you help your group work out the best way to show what Nikki was going through as you created your tableaux?

- I can use dramatic techniques to put together a story and act in role.

  Self-check: Did you draw on past drama work to help you use body language and expression effectively?

- I can evaluate how effective using different dramatic techniques has been.

  Self-check: Could you explain which tableau you thought was most effective and suggest how improvements could be made?

Build your skills

Use the skill steps below to help develop the dramatic techniques you use in preparing a performance of the following extract from *No Angels*. Here, Nikki is staying in a squat with three other homeless young people: Demi, River and Monkey.

I look from Monkey to River. Do you mean … you mug people for their phones? But that's …

Dishonest? supplies Monkey. What business isn't dishonest, Niks?

… If it weren't for us, the phone industry'd probably collapse.

They're all watching to see how I'll take it. I stare at the carpet between my toes, hearing the scrape of River's match as he lights up. They're untidy, the smokes he rolls, lumpy. He takes a drag, passes the cigarette to Monkey. Everyone's waiting.

I lift my eyes to Demi. She's finished her coffee, she's rolling the empty mug between her palms, not looking at me. Stock control, I murmur. Whose stock, Demi?

She smiles slowly, gazing at the mug. You've lived on the proceeds kiddo, received stolen goods. You're no different from the rest of us.

Step 1   Decide what ideas and information are in the text

1   Working in a group, reread the extract and use the questions below to help you work out what you want to show your audience in each part of your performance.

- What is happening?
- Who is speaking? How do they feel about the situation?
- What has happened before? What will happen next?

Step 2   Use dramatic techniques to explore the ideas

You are now going to prepare your dramatic performance of the scene. It must begin and end with a tableau – one revealing what has led up to this moment and the other showing how you think Nikki will respond to her discovery about the people she is living with.

1 a) Working in your group, prepare your performance, including opening and closing tableaux. Use the following questions to help you to think about the dramatic techniques you can use:

- **How will you use gestures and movement?** e.g. Nikki could hold out her open hands to Demi as if she is pleading with her.

- **What facial expressions should each character use?** e.g. Nikki might be frowning and look anxious and worried.

- **How should each character's voice sound as they speak?** e.g. Nikki might sound scared, but Demi's voice would be sneering.

b) Decide what will go in each part of your performance: the opening tableau, the dramatic reading and the closing tableau. Then practise your performance, taking care to include the different techniques you have agreed.

Step 3 Evaluate your performance

1 a) Working with another group, take it in turns to perform your tableaux and dramatic readings.

b) As you watch the other group's performance, use a chart like the one below to help you evaluate and comment on how effective you think this was. Then take it in turns to share your evaluations.

Stage in the performance	What techniques were used? (expression, gesture, voice, movement, etc.)	Evaluation (What did this make the audience think? What worked well? Why? What could be improved? Why?)
Opening tableau	River's expression is really innocent, but the way his hand is pulling the phone out of the man's pocket looks really sneaky ...	Showing this makes the audience realise River's very clever at this. He's making sure no one would guess what he was up to.
Dramatic reading	River sounds ...	
Closing tableau	Nikki's face shows she is feeling ...	

Reinforce your skills

One technique that can help you to explore what a character is thinking and feeling is called role-on-the-wall. This is where you draw an outline of a character and jot down notes inside to help you explore the problem and think about the character's viewpoint on it.

In the part of the story you have just read, the problem Nikki faces is that she has realised she is living in a squat with thieves. She doesn't want to become a criminal but is too young to get a job or to claim benefits. If she goes to a homeless shelter they will send her home.

1   Work in pairs. Prepare your **role on the wall** making notes about the way you think she would feel about:

- being homeless
- stealing
- Demi, River and Monkey.

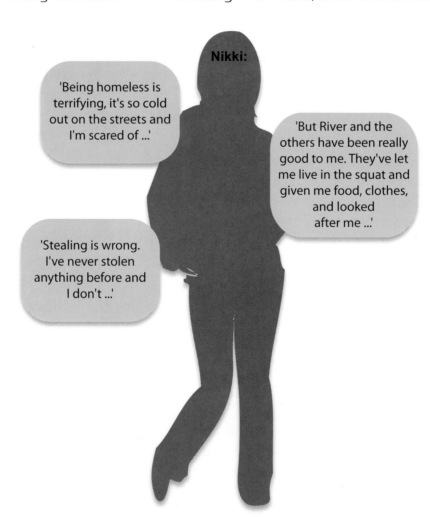

Nikki:

'Being homeless is terrifying, it's so cold out on the streets and I'm scared of ...'

'But River and the others have been really good to me. They've let me live in the squat and given me food, clothes, and looked after me ...'

'Stealing is wrong. I've never stolen anything before and I don't ...'

2   Use the ideas you have jotted down in your role on the wall to help you improvise a conversation between Nikki and Demi, River or Monkey. In this conversation, Nikki should decide whether she should carry on living in the squat or leave and try to find another way of surviving.

Stretch

Prepare a moment in your pair's improvisation when the action freezes (as in a tableau) but your character steps forward and speaks directly to the audience. Your character should explain how they feel and their behaviour. The action should then continue as if you had never spoken.

Extend your skills

Another dramatic technique you can use to show your understanding of a character and the issues they face is creating a video diary. You act in role as the character and explain your thoughts and feelings about events you have experienced. To do this well, you need to think about:

- what it is like to be that character
- what their point of view will be
- how the events will make him or her think or feel and how you can show this.

1   a)   Read this summary of the end of the story.

Nikki decides to stay in the squat with River and the others. Ronnie, her mother's partner, finds out she is living there and sets fire to the squat hoping to kill Nikki so that she cannot give evidence in a court case against him. Nikki and the others escape and are taken to hospital. Nikki tells the police that Ronnie started the fire. Her mother comes to see her and tells Nikki she knows the truth about Ronnie and apologises. Nikki decides to return home to live with her mother and sister. Ronnie is caught, and sent to prison for his crimes.

b)   Working in a group of three prepare a one-minute video diary, each taking the role of one of the characters (Nikki, Ronnie or River) and showing how they feel about and react to the events at the end of the story.

Support

Remember to show what your character is feeling and what they are like by using gestures, facial expression, voice and movement.

Apply your learning

Task Working in a pair, prepare and improvise a conversation between Nikki and her mother after she returns home. They should discuss what Nikki has done and why she made her choices. Your improvisation should begin and end with tableaux showing how the characters feel.

1 Use the 'role in the wall' technique to work out what each character might be thinking and feeling. Then prepare your performance: you need to use body language, gestures, movements and voice to show what is happening and the characters' thoughts and feelings.

2 Once you have given your improvisation, answer these questions to evaluate your performance:

- How did your preparation help you understand how the characters felt and how you could show this?

- What techniques did you use to get your ideas about Nikki and her mother across to your audience?

Assess to Progress

How confident are you now about using different dramatic techniques to help you explore ideas about a situation, character or issue? Look back at your original ratings on page 35 and decide where you would now place yourself on the scale. Use what you have learnt about yourself while taking part in the final activity to support your decisions and explain your reasons to a partner.

The charity Childline has visited your school to talk about the problem of teenagers running away from home. To help you think about this issue role-play a conversation between a teenager who is thinking of running away and a homeless person who is living on the street. In your role play, try to explain what life is like when you are homeless and what someone could do instead of running away from home.

Speaking and Listening AF6
Progress in ... Exploring language variation

- Investigate how the way people speak varies in different places and situations.
- Investigate how the way people speak changes with time.
- Use what you know about the ways language can vary to make effective choices about how to speak in different situations.

Activate your learning

1 Working in a group, try to sort the words and phrases below into three categories.

- Words used by people from different regions, e.g. Scotland, Newcastle.
- Words used in the past, e.g. by your grandparents or in the time of Shakespeare.
- Words which have come into English from another language, e.g. American slang.

> Something wicked this way comes ...

wee bairn   fuddy duddy   dag

the barbie   corny

alas and alack   daps

2 Now try to add five different words or phrases to each category. Do you all agree on which category different words should go in?

Assess to Progress

How good are you at understanding that how people speak varies in different places, situations and times? Do you use what you know to help you speak in different situations? Rate yourself for each of the skills below by deciding which number on the scale best shows your skill level.

| 1 | 2 | 3 | 4 | 5 | 6 | 7 |

I find this difficult.   I'm getting there.   I'm good at this.

● I can explore the language people use in their speech and explain how spoken English changes with time and varies in different regions.

   Self-check: Can you spot the different dialect words that characters in soap-operas such as *EastEnders* and *Neighbours* use?

● I can use my understanding of how language can vary to help me make the best choices when I speak in different situations.

   Self-check: Do you know how to speak in standard English in more formal situations?

Build your skills

Speech and language vary from region to region. Use the skill steps below to help you to investigate how language varies in this way.

Step 1   Collect examples of the way people speak

1   Working as a group, think about what you know about the **dialect words** used in different areas, such as London or Yorkshire and different countries, such as Australia or America. Think about the television programmes you watch where people use dialect words. Make a list of as many as you can and write an explanation of what each one means,

   e.g. Characters in *Neighbours* use Australian dialect words such as 'arvo' which means afternoon and 'daks' which means trousers.

2   Keep a speaking and listening diary. For a week record examples of spoken English from different regions, for example, characters', speech from your favourite soap or an interview with an American band on the radio. At the end of the week compare your diary with a partners, and discuss the examples you have found and how they are different.

Step 2 Think about the effects these examples have

It is important to understand the choices that speakers make and how they can use words to create specific **effects**.

1 Look back at the list you created and discuss what effect each example would have, e.g. would they make a speaker sound informal, modern or old-fashioned?

Reinforce your skills

The language people choose varies depending on the situation they are in (**setting**) and who they are speaking to (**context**).

1 Working in pairs, compare the language the Queen uses in the following transcripts. Think about these questions:

● what is different about the two situations?

● what is different about the type of English she uses?

● why does the Queen makes these language choices?

Transcript A

My Lords and Members of the House of Commons, My Government will pursue policies aimed at meeting the challenges which the United Kingdom faces at home and abroad. A stable economy is the foundation of a fair and prosperous society. My Government will continue to maintain low inflation, sound public finances and high employment. At the heart of my Government's programme will be further action to provide strong, secure and stable communities, and to address the threat of terrorism.

Transcript B

Sportsman: Can you play?

Queen: I've tried. I can't do the sort of things you do. No.

Sportsman: I'll have to coach you. Is that ok?

Queen: I don't think my brain works quick enough to do that – the speed of it.

Language

Stretch

Work through both transcripts picking out any examples of formal or informal English that you can identify. Try to explain why you think these are used and what impact they have on the audience. Think about the way the Queen addresses her audience and the vocabulary she chooses.

2 Working in pairs, discuss in which situations you change the way you speak. What changes do you make? Why?

Extend your skills

There are different reasons why the spoken language people use changes over time, for example new words can enter our vocabulary from other countries.

1 Working with a partner, make three lists:

   a) Fruit and vegetables that only grow in other countries, e.g. oranges, bananas, melons.

   b) Dishes that you enjoy eating which come from different cultures, e.g. chicken tikka masala.

   c) Music styles that you know which come from different places, e.g. reggae.

Something wicked this way comes …

2 Choose one word from each list. Investigate where the word came from and how it entered the English language.

New words also enter the language when new inventions and situations need new words to describe them.

3 Which of the following terms do you think have only been used in the last 75 years? Why?

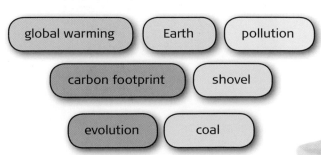

global warming   Earth   pollution

carbon footprint   shovel

evolution   coal

Language

The creative way in which people use words also means that word meanings can change, e.g. the word 'wicked' originally meant 'evil' but in the late 20th century it was adopted by teenagers as slang to mean 'brilliant'.

4 Investigate how the meanings of the following words have changed over time.

silly   awful   pretty   brave   nuisance

Apply your learning

Task Look at the following situation and think about the language used by the different people involved. Then complete the questions on the next page.

Doggy ... woof woof. Naughty doggy. Car go bang!

She was yakking away on one of those mobile phones. That's why she hit the lamp post. Some fusspot of a copper asked me what I'd seen but I just kept mum and said I'd been too busy wiping muck off the baby's pram to see anything.

She said she was on her way to her mam's when she seen this mutt come running into the road straight at her. Course she swerved like. She missed the dog but hit the lamp post. The car's a write off innit?

The dog, owned by Cerys Nugent of 21 Elkin Avenue, Splott, Cardiff, proceeded to run out into the road where it was in front of the vehicle. The driver swerved to the left in order to avoid hitting the animal, but in doing so came into contact with a lamp post.

Language

1   Investigate the language used in each of the speech bubbles.

   a)   How does the way each person speaks vary? Pick out any examples of dialect words used and explain what meaning they have.

   b)   Explain why these people speak in such different ways.

   c)   What effects do the language choices of each speaker have? Who sounds most official in this situation? Why?

2   a)   Working in a pair, role-play a policeman interviewing each witness to the accident to find out what actually happened. To do well, you need to think carefully about the way each person speaks at the time of the accident and how each person would speak while being interviewed.

   b)   After you have completed the role plays, write a commentary explaining the language choices you made and how you varied the way you spoke to make each character believable.

3   Look back at your speaking and listening diary. Choose three examples of spoken English you have found from different regions and explain how and why each one varies from language you use.

Assess to Progress

Think about the tasks you have completed in this unit. How good are you now at understanding how the way people speak varies in different places, situations and over time? Look back at the scale on page 42. Rate yourself again for each of the skills by deciding which number on the scale now shows your skill level best. Find examples from the work you have just completed to help justify the rating you give.

SKILLS FOR LIFE

Your school has set up an after-school advice centre where pupils can come for help from older pupils with any problems they might have in school. You have been asked to give advice to a new pupil who is worried about doing well in a maths test. Working with a partner, discuss what advice you could give the pupil and then role-play the conversation.

Speaking and Listening
Assessing your Progress

- Develop more complex ideas when you speak.
- Use a mixture of formal and informal speech.
- Use dramatic conventions and techniques to develop and sustain a role.
- Use what you know about the way language can vary to make effective choices about how to speak in different situations.
- Ask questions and prompt people to develop what they say.
- Make sustained contributions in discussions.

Working through this unit will give you the opportunity to show the progress you have made in your speaking and listening skills. You will complete three tasks where you will have the chance to show your skills in talking to others, to perform and with others.

Activate your learning

A travel agency called *Beyond the Imagination* is offering the following holidays:

> ⬩ **Lunar Leisure Week:** Travel by space shuttle to spend seven days on a space station experiencing life as an astronaut and enjoying stunning views of the Earth. Day trips include visiting famous parts of the moon, including the Sea of Tranquility.
> ⬩ **Working Wonders:** Make a real difference to someone's life by spending a month working to support a community in Africa, South America or China. Transform some waste land or dig a well. What better way to experience a country than to live with locals, sampling their food, but also leaving a lasting benefit to their community?
> ⬩ **Lights, Camera, Action:** A short break with a difference. Not only will you tour the film studios and real locations where your favourite TV programmes are set, you will rehearse with the cast and star in the episode they are filming.

1 Working in a group of four, decide which of these holidays you would most like to go on. Discuss what other information a tourist would need about the holiday, e.g. how you would travel, where you might stay, what the food would be like and additional activities.

2 At the end of your discussion, look at the list of different roles in a group on page 26. Which of these roles do you think you took in the discussion?

Progress task 1: Talking to others

A travel company is creating a series of travelcasts – short podcasts about holidays for tourists to download to their MP3 players to persuade them to choose that holiday.

Create a short podcast for the holiday of your choice.

Assess to Progress

In this task you will be assessed on the way you:

● organise your ideas so that what you say is logical for the listener

● use formal and informal language and other language effects to persuade and engage the listener

● use your voice to keep the listener interested.

The activities that follow will help you to create your podcast.

1   How formal should your podcast be? Consider these points and decide whether they indicate that the podcast should be formal or informal.

   ● It needs to feel friendly and welcoming.

   ● Young people are the most likely to listen to a podcast.

   ● It needs to be persuasive and sound convincing.

   ● The listeners will not be known to you.

   ● It needs to engage the interest of the listener.

   ● Your information needs to be clear for a range of listeners.

You are going to listen to a short podcast about travel to Australia.

2   Listen to the first section and discuss how it persuades the listener to book a trip to Australia.

G'day and welcome to travelcast Australia! I'm Marcus, a tour leader with Dream Travel Worldwide, and today I've got the job of giving you mouth-watering information about destinations in Australia. It's a unique place with so many unusual – and sometimes scary - animals that you just don't see anywhere else in the world, and it is absolutely massive, so you probably won't get to see it all in one go. Well, after all, it is a whole continent! It has got so much to entertain every visitor, whether you want relaxing sea and surf, famous sites like the mysterious Uluru and the stunningly beautiful Great Barrier Reef or to experience traditional Aboriginal culture. And, of course, it has fantastic weather, almost guaranteed. Tempted? Let's hear some details…

3 Now listen to the rest of the podcast. As you listen, make notes about the skills the speaker uses so you can answer the following questions:

- What sort of information does the speaker give and how is it organised?

- How formal or informal is the language?

- Does the speaker use any other language techniques to persuade the listener?

- How does the speaker use his voice to engage the listener?

Share your notes with a partner. How many different techniques did you notice?

4 Plan your own podcast about a holiday destination of your choice. It could be somewhere you have been recently or a place you would like to go to.

a) Create a list of the key places you will talk about and make a few notes about each of them.

b) Think about the viewpoint of your listeners: what do you think different people would want to know?

c) What other information can you give to interest your listeners? For example, do you know any interesting stories about the places you mention?

5 Now think about the way you need to speak and the rhetorical techniques you will use. How formal does the podcast need to be? Make a note of some phrases that you could use to capture the right tone and be persuasive. Think about using:

- repetition to emphasise a point

- pronouns, e.g. 'you', to involve the listener directly

- figurative language, e.g. similes or metaphors, to exaggerate or for a touch of humour

- adjectives to describe places in a positive way.

6 Think about how you are going to organise your ideas. Plan the introduction and ending. Getting the tone right at this point is really important to ensure your listeners keep listening! You could have:

- a general introduction

- sections giving details about each of the highlights of the trip (Think about how to link these sections together using connectives like 'firstly', 'after that' or 'on the other hand'.)

- an ending that is memorable or persuasive.

You could also add some brief comments from previous travellers or from the travel company to give a more personal view.

7 Now you are ready to read out or record your podcast. When you have completed the task, use this list of skills to assess a partner's podcast.

- What techniques were used to organise the podcast?

- Was the podcast spoken in a formal or informal way?

- What other language techniques did they use?

- How did they use pace, tone and volume to keep the listener interested in what they were saying?

As you listen, make notes on particular features you think worked well. Be ready to explain one point that you think they could improve.

Progress task 2: Talking to perform

You are a holiday-maker travelling in a group on one of the holidays listed on page 47. The group you are travelling with are from all parts of the UK. Working in groups of three or four, you are each going to adopt the role of one character.

Improvise a group video diary for one event on the holiday.

Assess to Progress

In this task you will be assessed on the way you:

- use dramatic conventions and techniques to develop and sustain a role

- use what you know about how language can vary to make effective choices about how to speak in different situations.

1. a) In your group, each take the role of a different holiday-maker on your chosen trip, e.g. a celebrity, a student, a scientist ...

   b) Agree on an event to talk about in the video diary and plan the details of the holiday that the holiday-makers are going to talk about. Remember, this will be information about what they did or saw, but also their feelings about it.

   c) Share some ideas about how each character might speak. Use these questions to guide you:

      ● Where are they from? Try to think of a few non-standard English words they might use.

      ● How old are they? Make some notes about what this means about the way they will speak.

      ● This is a video diary, so it will be quite informal. Think about how to use voice, movement and gestures to enhance the presentation.

2. To help you create your character and think about the language they use, create a role on the wall. Draw an outline of a person. Inside the shape, write notes about how they might feel. Outside the shape make notes about what others think of them and things that might happen to them. Select your ideas from the lists you create.

3. a) Spend a few minutes planning how you are going to organise the diary. Who will speak first? Will you all improvise in turn or will you sometimes talk as a group or in pairs?

   b) Practise your video diary. While each character improvises their part of the diary, the rest of the group need to listen for any language features that help to create the personality of the character.

   c) When you have finished, share your feedback with the group and identify what was different about the way different characters spoke. Use this information to improve your improvisation and perform your group video diary for the class.

4 Which statement below do you think best describes your performance in this task?

I spoke and acted in role, creating and maintaining a character through voice, gesture and movement.	I sustained my chosen role by adapting my voice, gestures and movements appropriately for the character and situation.	I sustained and adapted my role to show insight into the ideas and issues.
I sometimes used my knowledge of differences in spoken language to create the character I was role-playing.	I used my knowledge of differences in spoken language most of the time to deliberately change my speech to create the character I was role-playing.	I consistently used my knowledge of differences in spoken language to adapt my speech and create a convincing character.

Progress task 3: Talking with others

Fair Deal is a television programme that campaigns for consumers to be treated fairly by companies. One of the presenters is going to interview the director of a travel company that has sold holidays that failed to deliver what they promised.

Conduct an interview with the travel company director for the next show.

Assess to Progress

In this task you will be assessed on the way you:

- make sustained contributions in discussion, illustrating and explaining your ideas
- make suggestions in order to solve problems and test ideas
- ask questions that identify main points and prompt people to develop what they are saying
- challenge points people are making and ask for clarification.

Fair Deal has received several complaints from customers of the *Beyond the Imagination* travel company. Here are a few of them:

> On a recent Lunar Leisure holiday experience, one group of holiday-makers had less experience of space than expected when their shuttle flight failed to get off the ground. Several other holiday-makers have reported that the trips to the Moon did not go ahead and they ended up spending the whole week in the space centre. Some were offered a space walk instead but, at 73, the elderly couple concerned felt that was too risky.

> A group of gap-year students on a Working Wonders trip to Africa found themselves stranded in a remote village when the vehicle hired to take them back to the airport broke down just a mile from the village. They had already built a school room and had time to dig a well to give the children fresh water before the travel company managed to get them home.

> Lights, Camera, Action! hopefuls were disappointed with their week filming with their favourite TV stars when their accommodation turned out to be cold caravans in the studio car park.

In pairs, one of you will be the television interviewer and the other will be the director of the travel company.

1 Read the notes below about the different roles in the interview. Check that you understand them and add other ideas that you have.

Interviewer	Director
You want to find out what went wrong on these trips and what the company is going to do about it.	You want to make sure your company's image isn't damaged and will be keen to talk about all the successful trips you have run.
You may need to challenge what the director is saying.	You will be able to offer some sort of compensation to the people who had their holidays ruined.
Make sure that you deal with the issues above but you might have discovered some other problems too.	Keep pointing out all the good experiences people have had with your travel company. You could give some specific examples.
You need to listen to the director's answers and make your next question fit what you have just heard.	Think of ways you can turn negatives into positives in your answers.
You might need to ask questions in different ways, e.g. making a statement and asking the director what they think of that.	Try to extend your answers to give yourself more time to explain the good things you do by adding anecdotes or statistics.

2 Now think about your task.

a) Make brief notes on the questions you are going to ask or the points you are going to make. You only have six minutes of air time for the interview, so you will need to plan carefully.

- Look at the list of complaints. Decide how you are going to introduce or explain each one.

- Are there any other cases or examples of satisfied customers?

- What solutions do you want or can you offer?

b) Decide how you are going to speak in role and what movements or gestures will help you put your points across.

3 In pairs, conduct the interview between the director of the holiday company and the presenter. When you have completed the task, swap roles. Then discuss which role you think you played best and why. Use the Assess to Progress box on page 52 to remind yourself of the skills you needed to use.

Assess to Progress

You have completed three tasks: talking to others, talking to perform and talking with others.

Decide what skills you have used and the progress you have made.

Rate yourself for each skill by deciding which number on the scale below best shows your skill level.

1		3	4	5	6	7

I find this difficult.   I'm getting there.   I'm good at this.

- When talking to others, I can develop more complex ideas and use a mixture of formal and informal speech.

- When improvising I can use dramatic conventions and techniques to sustain a role.

- When talking with others, I can make sustained contributions in discussions and ask questions that help people to develop what they say.

Progress in ...
Reading

Progress in ... Reading and engaging with texts

LEARNING OBJECTIVES

- Develop the reading strategies you use to help you explore texts more fully.
- Express your preferences and opinions about texts effectively.
- Build a view of yourself as a reader, reflecting on your experiences of reading a wide range of texts.

Activate your learning

How have your reading tastes changed over time? Which books, magazines or comics did you read when you were younger? Which types of text do you read most often now?

1   Make a flow chart showing how your reading tastes have changed over time. You could use the format below to help you organise your ideas, but you can add extra details to this. Make sure you think about **all** the different types of text you have read, e.g. novels, non-fiction books, magazines, comics, websites and so on.

> My first reading memory is ...

> The first books I enjoyed reading were, e.g. I loved *Bob the Builder* magazine and the *Kipper* stories ...

> The types of book and magazine I read when I was at primary school included ...

> The types of book and magazine I read now are ... → I also read ...

> I like these because ...

2   Working in a group of four, discuss the different types of texts you have read this year. Don't just think about the books you have read in school – you should also think about magazines, websites or other texts that have stuck in your mind.

   a) Which text did you enjoy the most? Explain why you enjoyed it.

   b) Which text did you enjoy the least? Give reasons why you did not enjoy it. Remember to include any texts that you struggled with or didn't complete.

      e.g. It was a leaflet about how to look after the environment .... The information was presented in a confusing way and I couldn't keep track of it.

3   Look back at your flow chart. How have your reading habits changed? How do the texts you read at school differ from those you read at home?

Assess to Progress

Good readers know how to use different reading strategies to help them really get under the surface of a text and understand it more fully. How many of the following reading strategies do you use?

Make predictions	Speculate	Ask questions
Visualise	Hear a character's voice	Empathise

1   Working with a partner, complete the chart, sorting the reading strategies into the appropriate category.

Category	Strategies
A: I have used this strategy, I can explain how to read like this and I know why it is useful.	
B: I think I know how to use this strategy but I don't use it very often.	
C: I'm not sure what this reading strategy is and I'm not very confident about using it.	

2   Working as a class, share what you know about the different reading strategies. If you have put a reading strategy in category A, you should act as an expert and share what you know with people who have put the same strategy in categories B or C.

Build your skills

You are going to use reading strategies to explore the information that the publisher's website gives about the novel *The Shade of Hettie Daynes* by Robert Swindells.

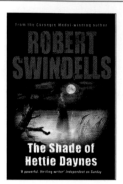

If you expect to see a ghost, you see a ghost …

That's what Bethan tells herself when her brother Harry takes her to see the ghost at the old reservoir. But she really *can* see it: a pale figure floating over the water, one finger pointing downwards. Local legend says that the ghost is the shade of Hettie Daynes, an ancestor of their family, who vanished over a hundred years ago. If so, what does she *want*? And why is she appearing now?

A deliciously shivery ghost tale from multi award-winning author Robert Swindells

Strategy 1 Make predictions and speculate

Making predictions means using what you already know to help you work out what to expect and what might happen next. Look at these three questions which can help you to make predictions.

- **What do I already know?**

  The cover shows a woman in old-fashioned clothes standing on water. The blurb talks about Bethan and Harry seeing a ghost called Hettie Daynes who is their ancestor but disappeared a long time ago.

- **What do I know from reading other texts like this?**

  I've read a story about ghosts which was creepy and had a twist at the end.

- **What do I think is going to happen in this text?**

  I think Bethan and Harry are going to try to find out what the ghost is trying to show them but it will be a trap.

Speculating means thinking of different possibilities, e.g. about what might happen next. You don't have to just rely on the evidence you have.

1   Speculate about why Hettie Daynes may have vanished.

Support
Using the following phrases can be helpful when you speculate:

- I wonder whether …
- Perhaps she might …
- Maybe she …
- It could be that …

Strategy 2 Ask questions

Asking questions as you read can help you to think about what is happening and the reasons why. You can then **read backwards and forwards** to help you find the answers. Look at the following example.

> When I started reading I wondered, 'Why is the ghost appearing to Bethan and Harry?' Reading backwards suggests it's because they expect to see a ghost, but reading forwards suggests it's because she's their ancestor.

2   Read the rest of the blurb. Write down two more questions you would like to ask. Can you find the answers in the blurb or on the cover?

Strategy 3 Visualise

Making a picture in your head of what is being described can help you think about where the characters are, what they can see and how they would be feeling.

> e.g. If Bethan can see the ghost standing on the water she must be nearby on the shore – perhaps peering through some plants, like the view on the cover.

3   Design an alternative cover based on the image you have visualised from the blurb.

Strategy 4 Hear a character's voice

As you read, try to **hear the characters' voices** in your head. This can help you to work out how they are feeling. Look at this example.

> Before Bethan sees the ghost she says, 'If you expect to see a ghost, you see a ghost.' I think she would say this in quite a calm way as if she doesn't believe that there actually is a ghost there.

4   How do you think Bethan would say: 'What does she want? And why is she appearing now?'? How does she feel about the ghost now?

Strategy 5 Empathise

To **empathise** means to imagine you are in the same situation as a character. This can help you to understand what they are thinking or feeling.

5   How do you think Harry feels when Bethan says, 'If you expect to see a ghost, you see a ghost'? Complete the following answer.

> If I was Harry I'd be angry that she didn't believe me – I'd want to …

Reinforce your skills

Now read the opening of the novel opposite. Use the reading strategies you explored in the previous section to help you complete the tasks.

1   Discuss with a partner what questions you would like to ask about the text. Then reread the text carefully to try to find the answers.

2   Predict what you think is going to happen next. Then join with another pair to share your predictions.

Support

Predictions should be made using details that are already there in the text. For example:

Bethan believes the ghost exists now and wonders whether it can see people, so she might go back and try to talk to it.

This example gives a detail from the text and then explains what you can predict from this.

3   Visualise the scene at the lake. Draw and label a diagram showing where Bethan, Harry and the ghost are, including as much detail as possible.

4   a) Working in a pair, prepare to act out a reading of the text. Before you start your reading, work out where in the text the characters feel any of the following emotions:

| frightened | amazed | calm | impatient | amused | confident |

   b) Think about how each character's voice should sound as they speak their lines.

   c) Join with another pair and take it in turns to act out your reading of the text. As you listen to the other pair's reading, make a note of any differences in the way they showed characters' feelings in their voices. Then discuss your reasons for making those different choices.

   e.g. You showed Harry feeling scared when he says ... but we think he feels ... because in the story it says ...

5   If you were Bethan, what would you feel and think on the way back home from the lake? Discuss your ideas with a partner.

6   Working in a group of four, speculate about why you think the ghost has started to appear again.

Harry squeezed his sister's arm. 'Are you sure you want to see her?'

Bethan snorted. ''Course. Wouldn't be here if I didn't, would I?'

The boy shrugged. 'Want you to be sure, that's all. She's seriously spooky, and you are only ten.'

'So? You're two years older, big deal.'

'OK, come on.'

The moon was nearly full, but there was mist over Wilton Water. Gorse grew thickly on this part of the bank. They halted, peering through prickly boughs. Their breath was like smoke on the cold October air.

'Is she there?' whispered Bethan.

'Hard to tell in this mist.'

'Bet she isn't. My teacher says there's no such thing as a ghost.'

Harry nodded. 'Yeah well, your teacher's never been to look, has she? Loads of people've seen her. Sensible people.'

Bethan shook her head. 'Mum hasn't, and she's lived here for ever.'

Harry sighed. 'Mum refuses to believe in ghosts, full stop. Look.' He pointed.

'Where, I can't see anything.'

'See that sapling on the bank over there?'

'Yes.'

'Well, look a little bit to the right of it.'

Bethan peered through the haze, and gasped. A woman in a long black skirt was standing on the water, looking towards the bank.

'You see her now, don't you?'

'I see something,' croaked Bethan, 'but it looks like it's standing on water. Nobody can stand on water. It's a whatsit illusion.'

'Optical,' whispered Harry. 'But it's not, it's the ghost. Me and Rob've seen her five or six times, and she's always exactly the same. If it was an optical illusion, you wouldn't see it twice the same.'

'Why does she stand so still then?'

'How the heck do I know, I'm not a ghost.' Harry chuckled. 'If you think it's an optical illusion, why are you whispering, hiding behind a bush? Stand up, give it a shout, see what happens.'

Bethan shook her head. 'No.'

'No, 'cause you know it's a ghost. Mum doesn't believe 'cause she doesn't want to. Some people are like that about ghosts.'

Bethan stared at the phantom. She saw a woman pointing a long, pale finger at the water. Try as she might, she couldn't turn it into a tree stump, a twist of vapour or a blend of moonlight and shadow. And she did try. After all, thousands of people see something on Loch Ness and mistake it for a monster. If you expect to see a monster, she thought, you see one. And if you expect to see a ghost, you see a ghost.

'OK,' murmured Harry. 'You wanted to see her, and you have. I better get you home now, or Mum'll make a ghost out of me.'

Bethan turned to look back as they moved away. The figure stood as before. Where does she go in the daytime, she wondered. Can she see us? Does she know people come to gawp at her, and does she mind?

She didn't ask her brother these questions: didn't want to admit she believed, but lying in bed that night it was the ghost she saw when she stared up into the darkness, and when she screwed her eyelids shut the phantom was behind them, keeping her from sleep.

Extend your skills

Look at the poem 'Geography Lesson' by Brian Patten opposite. You are going to use different reading strategies to explore what the poem is about.

1   Working in a pair, set a quiz with five questions which can be answered only by carefully reading the poem. Swap your questions with another pair and try to answer their questions.

2   a) Turn the poem into a cartoon strip with six frames. Each frame should illustrate what the poet is showing readers in one stanza.

    b) Join with another pair. Compare your cartoons and discuss why you visualised the poem in different ways.

Stretch

How does the mood change through the poem? With your partner choose appropriate quotations from the poem to add as captions to your cartoon that help to show the mood in each stanza.

Once you have worked out what the poem is about, you can then start to **make judgements** about the text. Making judgements means giving your opinions about a text and supporting your opinions with evidence.

3   a) Do you like or dislike the poem? Do you think the characters are believable?

    b) Discuss your opinions with a partner. Explain what is in the text that has made you think or feel the way you do,

    e.g. I preferred the second stanza because I like the way the writer shows the difference between the 'grey' home of the geography teacher and the beautiful places he would like to visit.

4   Working in a group, discuss whether you preferred the poem or the opening of the novel that you read in the previous section. Listen to other people's opinions and give reasons to support your choice.

'I left school when I was 15, and when I was 14 there was this very wonderful teacher who covered his classroom in maps, and he always said when he retired from school, he would go to certain places on these maps.'

Brian Patten

Geography Lesson

Our teacher told us one day he would leave the school
And sail across a warm blue sea
To places he had only known from maps,
And all his life had longed to be.

The house he lived in was narrow and gray
But in his mind's eye he could see
Sweet-scented jasmine clambering up the walls,
And green leaves burning on an orange tree.

He spoke of the lands he longed to visit,
Where it was never drab or cold.
And I couldn't understand why he never left,
And shook off our school's stranglehold.

Then half-way through his final term
He took ill and never returned.
And he never got to that place on the map
Where the green leaves of the orange trees burned.

The maps were pulled down from the classroom wall;
His name was forgotten, it faded away.
But a lesson he never knew he taught
Is with me to this day.

I travel to where the green leaves burn,
To where the ocean's glass-clear and blue,
To all those places my teacher taught me to love –
But which he never knew.

Apply your learning

This is a diary entry written by Dennis, a driver who takes tourists on trips to watch polar bears in north-eastern Canada.

> 12 October
>
> Zero degrees, light south wind, overcast skies... No northern lights tonight, seems we will be missing out on quite a light show.
>
> Bears, bears, bears... I'm surrounded by bears, 13 ... 14 ... 15 and counting. An old friend is amongst them, Dancer showed up early the other morning, it was good to see him again. He didn't waste any time and got right into it with another large bear, standing toe to toe, battling and bumping like sumo wrestlers gone mad. There's also a mother with a set of first year cubs and a mother with a second-year cub make part of the gathering around camp. After a long bout of sparring the combatants like to cool off by flopping down on the ice or fresh snow, Dancer was doing just that when I turned the camera on him, resting as only he does, stretched out on his side with front paws crossed and back legs crossed when the Timber Wolf came into view.

GLOSSARY

sparring – pretend fighting, wrestling

combatants – fighters

Task

1   Make a diagram of the scene Dennis is describing, showing where he and each of the bears mentioned are.

2   Which of these statements best describes how Dennis feels about Dancer? Explain your answer.

   a Dennis is wary of Dancer.

   c Dennis enjoys watching Dancer sparring.

   b Dennis is impressed by Dancer's strength.

   d Dennis is horrified by Dancer's behaviour.

3   Look at the following quotations from the diary and, for each one, explain how Dennis was feeling at the time:

   a) 'no Northern Lights tonight, seems we will be missing out on quite a light show'

   b) 'Bears, bears, bears ... I'm surrounded by bears'

4   Based on what you have read so far, speculate on what Dancer will do next.

5   Would you like to read more of Dennis' diary? Explain your answer.

Assess to Progress

1   How confident are you now about using the range of reading strategies you have practised in this unit? Look back at the category you gave to each of the reading strategies on page 57. Which category would you put each of the strategies into now?

2   How confident are you at making judgements about a text? How easy do you find it to back up your opinions with evidence?

3   Think about all the work you have completed in this unit.

   a)   What have you learnt that you did not know or could not do before?

   b)   What was the hardest part of this unit?

SKILLS FOR LIFE

The school librarian has asked your advice about whether to buy this book for your library. Read the blurb and then answer the questions.

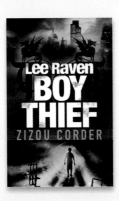

Lee Raven, boy thief, has stolen something he really didn't mean to. Now he faces a perilous flight through London as he tries to escape capture – because Lee has stolen the Book of Nebo, a book that has existed for thousands of years and tells every story and legend known to man. It's priceless. Some will even kill to possess it. The pressure mounts and the future of Nebo is in Lee's hands – can he prevent the most dangerous ending of them all?

1   Which words in the blurb makes this sound like an interesting book to read?

2   What section would you put this book in? Romance? Mystery? How can you tell?

3   Do you think the librarian should buy a copy of this book for your school, or not? Explain why.

Progress in ... Developing active reading strategies

LEARNING OBJECTIVES

- Use a range of reading strategies to locate information in print, electronic and multi-modal texts.
- Make relevant notes when gathering information from more than one text and compare and contrast the information you find.
- Distinguish between facts and opinions.
- Summarise the main points from a text.

Activate your learning

1   Working with a partner, scan the navigation box from the Girls Aloud website and decide where you would click to find the following information:

   a) Where would you find photographs of the girls?

   b) Where would you find information about their upcoming tour?

   c) Where might you find a Girls Aloud make up bag?

   d) Where would you find somewhere to talk to other fans?

   e) What do you think you would find if you clicked on 'GA Style'?

LOGIN ◯   ◯ sign up

home   the Girls   gallery   diary   GA Style   chat   music and videos   GA Club   Shop   sign up

GIRLS ALOUD

2   a) Now look at 'the Girls' section of the website on the next page. Skim-read this and decide what their most important achievement has been.

   b) Write a sentence of no more than 25 words summarising this section. Then share your sentence with another pair. Did you include the same points?

Girls Aloud

Girls Aloud, the UK's premier girl band are back with a brand new look, new single and a new album!

After five years, three albums and a Greatest Hits, Sarah, Nadine, Kimberley, Nicola and Cheryl have even entered the Guinness Book of Records for the girl group with the most ever consecutive top ten singles. Having beaten records set by both Destiny's Child and even the Spice Girls, the proven **Girls Aloud** will go down in history as one of the UK's most successful bands ever.

But the story doesn't end there. No, out on November the 19th 2007 is the Girls brand new album, Tangled Up. The first album full of original material since 2005's Chemistry. So, ignore the rumours, the Girls aren't going anywhere. 'We 100% love what we do,' **Nicola says**, 'Why would we quit now? We've just finished an ace new album and we're really proud of it. Just wait to see what we've got in store!'

Cheryl adds, 'The press always make up rumours that we're rowing or breaking up, but it's just so they can sell papers. It's just not true!'

It looks like 2008 is going to be another massive year for **Girls Aloud**!

3 Use your close-reading skills to decide whether the following statements about Girls Aloud are fact or opinion and find evidence to support your decision.

a) The band has had an incredibly busy five years.

b) They will be even more successful in the future.

c) The writer wants us to think they are a more popular band than Destiny's Child or the Spice Girls.

d) They will not split up in 2008.

Assess to Progress

How good are you at picking out the main points and finding the most relevant information from the different texts you read? Rate yourself for each skill by deciding which number on the scale below best shows your skill level. You will need to be able to justify your decisions, so try to think of examples that support your choice.

1	2	3	4	5	6	7

I find this difficult.　　　　I'm getting there.　　　　I'm good at this.

- I know how to use different strategies such as scanning, skimming and close reading to find information from the texts I read.

- I can sum up the main points from a text.

- I can tell the difference between facts and opinions.

- I know how to make effective notes when I am using more than one source of information and am able to compare and contrast the information I find.

Build your skills

Jessica has been offered a Staffordshire Bull Terrier puppy by her friend, whose family breed dogs. Jessica's mum has told her that she needs more information to convince her that this type of dog is safe before she will let her have the puppy. Jessica follows the steps below to research this.

Step 1   Use a range of sources

When you are doing research, try to use a range of sources to provide you with different views on the topic. Jessica has found three different sources of information using the library and the internet.

- *'Is a Staffordshire Bull Terrier the Correct Dog for you?'* An article from the Staffordshire Bull Terrier Breed Council web page.

- A description of the Staffordshire Bull Terrier from the Kennel Club.

- A government leaflet about the types of dog banned in Britain.

Jessica has created a table to help her decide how useful each source will be.

Source	Information I think this will give me	Positives	Negatives
'Is a Staffordshire Bull Terrier the Correct Dog for you?' – an article from the STB Breed Council webpage	It will tell me what kind of dog the Staffordshire Bull Terrier is and what kind of home is most suitable for this pet.	I know from the title it will include the information I want to find out. The person writing the article has many years of experience with this type of dog.	It may be biased in favour of Staffordshire Bull Terriers as it has been written by somebody who has a fondness for this type of dog.

1   Working with a partner, complete the table for the other two sources.

2   Join with another pair and discuss what other sources Jessica could use to find the information she needs. Add your ideas to the table. Think about the positives and negatives of using each source.

3 a) Discuss how reliable and how accurate you think each of the different sources of information you have listed is. Think about the following questions:

- Who has produced the information? Are they trustworthy and knowledgeable?

- Is the source balanced? Might it be biased towards one point of view?

- When was the source produced? Is the information up to date?

b) Give each source a reliability rating using a scale from 1 to 5, where 5 means very reliable and 1 means not reliable at all.

Step 2 Scaffold your research

Jessica used a KWEL grid to help her to scaffold and organise her research. This type of grid can remind you of what you are trying to find out as you read your different sources.

What do I already **know** about the topic?	What do I **want** to know about the topic?	Where will I find the **evidence?**	What have I **learnt?**
Staffordshire Bull Terriers have received a lot of bad press	Are they a dangerous pet?	Government leaflet about banned dogs	Staffordshire Bull Terriers are not banned

Another way of organising your research is to use a QuADS grid. QuADS grids can be useful when you want to pinpoint your research once you have decided on a specific focus.

Question	Answer	Detail	Source
Which dogs are good with children?	Staffordshire Bull Terrier	'Highly intelligent and affectionate, especially with children.'	Kennel Club description

1 Working with a partner, discuss which grids you have used before when researching topics. Have you used any other techniques to help you organise your research?

2 Which type of grid would be the most helpful if you wanted to:

a) research what type of dog you wanted to keep as a pet?

b) try to find out what kind of exercise your pet needs?

Step 3 Use reading strategies to identify and summarise key information

Using different reading strategies, Jessica has picked out the key points from the texts she has found. She knows her mum is busy so she has attached notes to each article summarising the key points. Look at the strategies she has used and the summaries she has made on the first two texts.

1   Using your own words, summarise the main points from the text on the opposite page. Try to include quotations from the text in the notes you make.

She has skim read and used the pictures to help her to check she has found the right texts.

She has scanned the text using the headings to find the right areas.

Types of dogs prohibited in Great Britain

This one's from the gov. It says SBTs are not on the banned list – only Pit Bulls.
The BBC website has info too.
♡ Jess x

Guidance on the recognition of prohibited dogs in Great Britain

About Defra
www.defra.gov.uk

defra
Department for Environment
Food and Rural Affairs

She has summarised the key information using abbreviations her mum will understand and has not written in full sentences.

Staffordshire Bull Terrier Breed Standard

© The Kennel Club – Unauthorised Reproduction of Text and Imag

The Kennel Club Picture Library – © D. Paton

General Appearance
Smooth-coated, well balanced, of great strength for his size. Muscular,

Characteristics
Traditionally of indomitable courage and tenacity. Highly intelligent and affec

Temperament
Bold, fearless and totally reliable.

Head and Skull
Short, deep though with broad skull. Very pronounced cheek muscles, disti   ort foreface, nose black.

Eyes
Dark preferred but may bear some relation to coat colour. Round, of medium size, and set to look straight ahead. Eye rims dark.

Ears
Rose or half pricked, not large or heavy. Full, drop or pricked ears highly undesirable.

Mouth
Lips tight and clean. Jaws strong, teeth large, with a perfect, regular and complete scissor bite, i.e. upper teeth closely overlapping lower teeth and set square to the jaws.

Neck
Muscular, rather short, clean in outline gradually widening towards shoulders.

Forequarters
Legs straight and well boned, set rather wide apart, showing no weakness at the pasterns, from which point feet turn out a little. Shoulders well laid back with no looseness at elbow.

Body
Close-coupled, with level topline, wide front, deep brisket, well sprung ribs; muscular and well defined.

Hindquarters
Well muscled, hocks well let down with stifles well bent. Legs parallel when viewed from behind.

Feet
Well padded, strong and of medium size. Nails black in solid coloured dogs.

Tail
Medium length, low-set, tapering to a point and carried rather low. Should not curl much and may be likened to an old-fashioned pump handle.

Gait/Movement
ree, powerful and agile with economy of effort. Legs moving parallel when viewed from front or rear. iscernible drive from hindlegs.

oat
nooth, short and close.

olour
d, fawn, white, black or blue, or any one of these colours with white. Any shade of brindle or any shade of ndle with white. Black and tan or liver colour highly undesirable.

e
irable height at withers 36-41 cms (14 to 16 ins), these heights being rel ed to the weights. Weight: dogs: 7 kgs (28-38 lbs); bitches 11-15.4 kgs.

lts

Mum,
This one's from the Kennel Club. It says SBTs are reliable & good with children – one of two recomm. breeds for kids. ♡ Jx

She has close read the article to pick out the key information looking for particular details that the writer has repeated.

Is a Staffordshire Bull Terrier the Correct Dog for you?

Before you buy a Staffordshire Bull Terrier puppy it is wise to ensure that this is the correct dog for you and your family. The Stafford is renowned for its affinity with humans and is particularly good with children. He is therefore a dog who is more comfortable sharing your home or indeed your lap, than spending long periods of time on his own in a kennel. It should be borne in mind that the cute little puppy you first brought home will mature into a powerful and muscular animal and, the males particularly, require a strong arm to control the lead. Staffords love human contact and will often be boisterous with visitors – you have to be prepared for the fact that not all your friends will appreciate this. Having a dog is a lot of extra work and responsibility and you need to be sure that you wish to commit yourself to your dog's welfare for its lifespan, which on average is between 10 -12 years.

Because of its close relationship with humans the Stafford does not make a good guard dog and is not suited to being left for long periods without outside stimulation. The Stafford has a colourful history and it is to be remembered that whilst they love people, they will react if challenged by another dog. For this reason you must always be a responsible owner and never take your dog into a public place unless he is on a collar and lead.

Of course there are many positive aspects of Stafford ownership – he is a dog with special qualities which makes him an ideal family dog. The Staffordshire Bull Terrier is well suited to a close living relationship with its human companions – he is highly intelligent and thrives on a one-to-one basis, being ever eager to please and he will give you a lifetime of devotion.

Reinforce your skills

When you are reading to find information, **close reading** skills can help you to explore what is fact and what is opinion. It is helpful to find more than one source and **compare** and **contrast** the information they give, e.g. note when a piece of information you find in one article is backed up by evidence in another.

Be careful: even if an opinion is repeated in many sources, this does not make it a fact. Often opinions are presented as fact. Read the articles on the next page, taken from *BBC News* magazine and the *Independent* newspaper. Complete the following activities to help you spot the **facts** and **opinions** given.

1   Working with a partner, closely read each of the highlighted statements in the first article and decide whether you think each one is a fact or an opinion.

2   Using the same reading strategy, identify all the facts in the second article. Think about how you could work out whether they are true.

3   Compare and contrast the two articles. Make a list of the points that are included in both articles and then note down the main differences.

4   Why are Staffordshire Bull Terriers being dumped by their owners? Use a QuADs grid to make notes that help you answer this question by reading the two articles.

5   Working with your partner, each of you should choose one of the articles and write a summary of it for Jessica's mother.

Ruff deal for the Staffie

They're being dumped in record numbers and branded a 'yob dog', yet Staffordshire Bull Terriers are ideal family pets, say experts. So why is this nation of dog lovers turning against them?

Extremely reliable, highly intelligent and affectionate, especially with children. It's not a description most of us would associate with Staffordshire Bull Terriers, but it's how the UK Kennel Club sums them up.

In fact, the breed is one of only two from over 190 it recommends as suitable with children, the other being a Chesapeake Bay Retriever.

But while the thought of a doe-eyed retriever makes people feel all warm and fuzzy inside, a Staffie – as they are commonly known – often leaves them cold.

So how did the sociable dog that likes to be loved fall out of people's affections?

The breed is a bit of a contradiction and that is a big part of the problem, says the Dogs Trust. While their natures are loving, their perceived physical similarities with banned breeds – such as Pit Bulls – has resulted in them being tarnished with the 'dangerous dogs' label.

'Because of their appearance, certain types of people think they've got themselves a fierce dog and in fact they'd far rather be in front of the fire having their tummy tickled,' says breeder Veronica Brown.

As a result of this misguided association they have become a 'macho' fashion accessory among some young men, say welfare groups. They are a 'pseudo Pit Bull' for those who want to look hard.

GLOSSARY

pugnacious – inclined to fight or quarrel

pseudo – appearing to be

How did the Staffordshire Terrier fall in with the wrong crowd?

The Staffordshire Terrier is fast becoming the weapon of choice for urban thugs.

It looks moody, tough and mean, and it loves a scrap: stocky, muscular, big head, strong jaws, and short, no-nonsense coat. Put a heavy studded collar on it, clip on a chromed chain-link lead, and it's the street-accessory of choice on estates across Britain. The Staffordshire Bull Terrier looks the part: uncompromisingly urban, hard as nails.

And now, 15 years after Pit Bull Terriers were banned under the Dangerous Dogs Act, reports from all sorts of sources – from dog-walkers to politicians – are warning that Staffordshires, Mastiffs and other pugnacious dog breeds are once again becoming the accessory – and occasionally the weapon – of choice on Britain's urban streets. Typical new breed of owner: young lad, aged 15–22. Typical purpose for having the dog: to gain respect, to intimidate, to use as a form of protection, and sometimes for crime.

It's the Staffordshire's misfortune that, of all breeds, it most closely resembles the fearsome Pit Bulls which, in the 1980s, were the favoured side-arm of drug dealers, hard men and general riff-raff alike. And, though if treated kindly and properly trained, Staffordshires are good with young children, they are feared.

'A lot of people look at them horrified, like you've got Satan himself on the end of your lead,' says Marian Waller from south London, owner of a Staffordshire Bull Terrier named Teddy. She adds, 'They'll cross the road to get away. I don't know why, because they're great with people. Like everyone else, she says the problem is not with the dogs but with some of the owners. 'It depends who's got them,' she says. 'They might be naff owners who bait them.'

Extend your skills

Samir has to complete a research project about why Stonehenge was built. He has used the following sources of information from the library and the internet.

About Stonehenge:

Age: estimated at 3100 BC
Location: Wiltshire, UK
Type of stone: Bluestone, Sarsen, Welsh Sandstone
Worship: lunar, solar

www.stonehenge.co.uk

It was generally concluded that Stonehenge was constructed as a temple to the sun. More recently, though, the astronomer Gerald Hawkins has argued that Stonehenge is not merely aligned with solar and lunar astronomical events, but can be used to predict other events, such as eclipses. In other words, Stonehenge was more than a temple, it was an astronomical calculator.

www.witcombe.sbc.edu/stonehenge/archeoastronomy.html

Stonehenge should best be regarded as a prehistoric temple, its scale of construction raising it far above the many other monuments constructed for a similar purpose.

Stonehenge by J. Richards

Stonehenge was the meeting place of a particularly powerful tribe, probably under the influence of several strong chiefs or chiefly dynasties, who could muster the manpower to build a permanent tribal centre. This was the symbol of one tribe's authority over others.

Stonehenge and the Origins of Western Culture by L.E. Stover and B. Kraig

Look at the closing paragraph of Samir's report summarising why Stonehenge was built.

> There are many different opinions about Stonehenge and the reasons it was built. Stonehenge has been seen as a temple or meeting place. Some people say it is a giant calculator or a giant calendar or even a site of sacrifice. Others think it was built by people from Atlantis who were also responsible for the pyramids in Egypt and Latin America.

1 a) Look back at the original information sources and find the evidence that supports what Samir has written. With a partner, discuss how Samir has put this information into his own words.

   b) What other key points could Samir have added to his paragraph based on the information he has read? Rewrite the paragraph in your own words including these additional points.

Stretch

What other sources of information could you use to find out more information about why Stonehenge was built? Which do you think would give you the most reliable information?

2 a) How do we know that Stonehenge was an important place when it was built? Reread the four texts, picking out the key information that helps you to answer the question.

   b) Summarise the information you have found in a paragraph of no more than 25 words.

   c) Compare your answer with a partner's. Have you both included the same key points?

Support

Use a support grid to help you collect and evaluate the information you find.

Key information	Source of information
Why do you know the information is relevant?	How do you know the source is reliable?

Apply your learning

Task Your friend is trying to choose the best way to exercise and keep fit. Your friend has not done much exercise before and wants to choose an activity that they can do on their own. You have found the following texts.

BRITISH CHEERLEADING ASSOCIATION

| Home | Safety & Rules | Information | Resources | Forms (All) | Suppliers Guide |

Cheerleaders are Athletes

Cheerleading involves **cheers**, **chants**, **jumps**, **dance**, **tumbling**, **gymnastics**, **partner stunts** and **pyramid building**. Cheerleaders are not just dance entertainers at games, they have to master difficult and demanding athletic techniques and be effective crowd leaders, often training longer hours than the players they cheer for. During a typical game, American football players may get breaks, but cheerleaders go flat out for three and a half hours in all weather.

Competitive Cheerleading

Already accepted as an **athletic discipline** in its own right in many countries, international cheerleading championships have up to **210 squads** competing and attract over 12,000 cheerleaders, family and friends. Some are televised on prime time sports channels.

Tackling the big one

by Andrew Hamilton, BSc Hons MRSC

How many truly remarkable things have you done in your life? If the answer is not many, or even none, then maybe it's time to run a marathon. Because no matter how fit you are, running 26.2 miles for the first time will certainly be one of the most memorable moments in your life. And while the marathon takes no prisoners, if you train intelligently and diligently, you can succeed and achieve something quite remarkable ...

Let's get one thing straight from the outset: running a marathon is not like running a longer version of a 10k fun run or half-marathon. Marathon running will push your body through physical and mental barriers, and as such needs to be treated with respect. Unlike most other running events, the marathon will find out weaknesses and punish those who are inadequately prepared!

http://www.onlineshop.com

The Ropeless Jump Rope! with 6 Weights & DVDs

Don't worry about tripping over ropes with this great rope-less skipping rope! It's a computerised jump rope with an LCD computer integrated in one of the two handles. Set jump targets and it will beep when you reach them. It also has a talk mode for a work-out summary, a two person memory for use with a friend, a stopwatch, timer and automatic shut off. It also includes six weights that you can insert into each handle. Use this item indoors or out for toning and cardio vascular excercise.

Comes with a carry bag and two AAA batteries.

Overall Rating ☆☆☆☆☆

1   Use the right reading strategy to read the texts on page 75 to help you find the answers to the following questions.

   a) How many squads can compete in international cheerleading championships?

   b) What distance is run in a marathon?

   c) What different functions does the LCD computer in the Jump Snap rope have?

2   Using the information in the articles, decide which of the following statements are fact and which are opinion.

   a) Cheerleading is an activity performed by boys and girls.

   b) If you don't adequately prepare for a marathon you will injure yourself.

   c) The Ropeless Jump Rope is great value as it also comes with DVDs.

3   Rank the three activities described in order of the level of fitness they require from the most to the least difficult. Find evidence to support your decision and pick out relevant quotations.

4   Your friend has asked you to send a summary of each article. Write a short email summarising the main points in each.

5   Which activity would you recommend to your friend? Write a paragraph giving reasons for your recommendation and explaining why you do not think the other two activities are suitable.

Assess to Progress

How good are you now at each of these skills?

- Using a range of reading strategies to find information from texts.

- Distinguishing between fact and opinion.

- Making relevant notes when gathering information from different texts and comparing and contrasting the information you find.

- Summarising the main points from a text.

Work with a partner. Look back at the ratings you gave yourself on page 67 and decide whether any of them should change. Use the work you have done in this unit to help you make your decisions.

SKILLS FOR LIFE

You are trying to find venues for your birthday party. Your mum has given you a budget of £200. You want to have an active day with something to eat afterwards. Use a range of strategies to read the the children's parties page of the Chill factor-e website below, then answer the questions.

1 Where would you look on the website to find out more information about what the luge and tubing activities actually are?

2 If you wanted to choose the luge party and all your friends are 12 or older, how many could you take with your budget?

3 Which activity would be most suitable for your younger cousins who are aged between four and seven years old?

4 Write a sticky note to your mum explaining which package you want to choose for your birthday party and summarising in your own words what this includes.

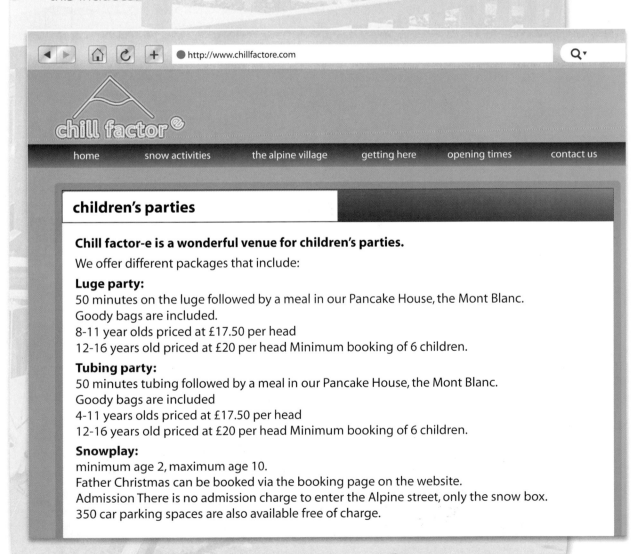

http://www.chillfactore.com

chill factor ©

home | snow activities | the alpine village | getting here | opening times | contact us

children's parties

Chill factor-e is a wonderful venue for children's parties.

We offer different packages that include:

Luge party:
50 minutes on the luge followed by a meal in our Pancake House, the Mont Blanc.
Goody bags are included.
8-11 year olds priced at £17.50 per head
12-16 years old priced at £20 per head Minimum booking of 6 children.

Tubing party:
50 minutes tubing followed by a meal in our Pancake House, the Mont Blanc.
Goody bags are included
4-11 years olds priced at £17.50 per head
12-16 years old priced at £20 per head Minimum booking of 6 children.

Snowplay:
minimum age 2, maximum age 10.
Father Christmas can be booked via the booking page on the website.
Admission There is no admission charge to enter the Alpine street, only the snow box.
350 car parking spaces are also available free of charge.

Reading AF3
Progress in ... Using inference and deduction

- Use inference and deduction to explore layers of meaning within a text.
- Develop your explanations of the inferences you make, drawing on evidence from across a text.
- Consider how details contribute to the overall meaning of a text.

Activate your learning

When you first look at a text, you need to be able to read it investigatively, using **inference** and **deduction** to work out what it is telling you. When you make an inference, you read beneath the surface of a text and use hints and clues to reach your own interpretation of what is happening. When you make a deduction you come to a conclusion based on the evidence.

1   Look at this picture. Working in a pair, try using your skills of inference and deduction as you discuss:

- the different things you can see in the picture

- what you can infer from the picture, e.g. what you think may have happened

- what you can deduce from the picture, e.g. when, where and what the picture depicts.

2 You can also use these skills when reading a text. Working with a partner, read this crime scene report and then answer the questions.

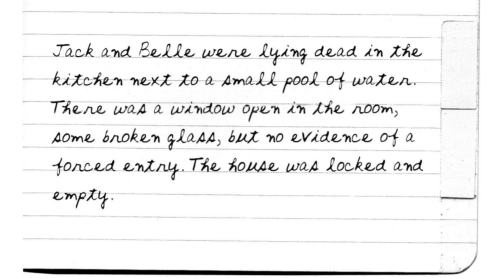

> Jack and Belle were lying dead in the kitchen next to a small pool of water. There was a window open in the room, some broken glass, but no evidence of a forced entry. The house was locked and empty.

a) What inferences can you draw about the setting?

b) What inferences can you draw about Jack and Belle?

c) What do you deduce has happened to them?

Remember to look carefully at the details included in the crime report to help you infer and make the right deduction.

Assess to Progress

How good do you think you already are at using inference and deduction? Rate yourself for each skill by deciding which number on the scale below best shows your skill level.

1   3   4   5   6   7

I find this difficult.   I'm getting there.   I'm good at this.

- I can use inference to explore layers of meaning.

- I can make deductions based on evidence.

- Using inference and deduction, I can explain possible meanings and interpretations.

Build your skills

Read the newspaper article below about floods in Britain. Think about the different strategies you could use to help you understand the text.

- **Questioning**: What is happening? Who or what is involved? Is this normal?

- **Visualising**: Create a picture in your mind of what is going on – what can you see?

- **Empathising**: Try to imagine how you would feel in a similar situation.

- **Predicting**: Use what you know to think about how the situation might develop.

The Environment Agency has warned further flash floods are expected

Families in flood-risk areas have been warned to expect heavy rain for another five days.

Forecasters said there would be no real let-up in the weather until next week. That prediction means river levels, already high after repeated deluges since Friday, could rise further. Homes and businesses left on the brink in some areas after fresh rain on Tuesday will be forced to wait behind their sandbags until Sunday at the earliest. A spokesman for the Environment Agency warned people to 'remain vigilant'.

The agency reported 68 flood warnings across the country on Tuesday, with a further 187 areas on flood watch. The Port of Dover was forced to close because of force nine winds in the Channel. It later reopened, with P&O Ferries and Sea France services to Calais and Norfolkline to Dunkirk subject to severe delays.

Areas affected by severe flooding earlier this year were particularly anxious. Laurence Robertson, MP for Tewkesbury, said it was wrong people were living 'on a knife edge' because of failures by the government.

'I don't think enough has been done. The fact people are really worried and living on a knife edge is not right. There are still hundreds living in caravans and they're nowhere near to moving back home,' he said.

Michael Dukes, forecast manager for Meteogroup, said surface water would have no chance to clear because of repeated downpours in the days ahead.

Daily Express, Tuesday January 15, 2008

Public Footpath Severn Way

Use the skill steps to explore the text, answering the questions as you do.

Step 1 Use reading strategies to help you to understand the text

Working with a partner, discuss what you now know about the situation described in the text.

1 What are we told are the main causes of the flooding?

2 Who is being affected by the flooding? How do they feel?

Step 2 Use clues to make inferences

1 Look closely at the words and phrases used as these can give you clues that help you to make inferences. Look back to find the following quotations in the article and use the questions to help you infer. The first one has been completed for you.

Quotation	Inference
'Homes and businesses left on the brink in some areas' What does this mean? What might they be 'on the brink' of? Have you heard this phrase used in any other situations?	This means things are at a critical point. If it continues raining, homes and businesses will definitely flood catastrophically.
'forced to wait behind their sandbags' What does the word 'forced' imply? What are they waiting for? Why might they need sandbags?	
'remain vigilant' What does the word 'remain' suggest about their situation? What does 'vigilant' mean? Why might they need to remain vigilant?	

2 Pick out any other quotations from the article that give you clues about how people feel about the situation described. Add these to the table and make inferences that explore what the quotations mean.

Step 3 Make deductions and explore the overall meaning

To make sure you understand the overall meaning of a text, you need to build up the inferences and deductions that you make from across the text. This means looking at the different clues and pieces of evidence and thinking about the overall effect that they give.

1   Look back at the quotations in your table. What do they suggest about how the people might be feeling?

2   Looking at all the inferences you have made, what do you think the flood situation is being compared with?

3   What can you deduce about how the writer wants the reader to feel about the situation?

Support

Use the following sentence starters to express your ideas.
- I think that the ... because ...
- It seems as if ... because ...
- At this point I noticed that ...
- It seemed as if the author wanted the reader to feel ... because ...

Stretch

1   What do you deduce from the following quotations?
- '68 flood warnings', 'across the country'
- '187 areas on flood watch'
- 'The Port of Dover was forced to close'
- 'people were 'living "on a knife edge"'
- 'hundreds living in caravans'

2   Now look at the quotation 'it was wrong people were living "on a knife edge" because of failures by the government.' Discuss with a partner what conclusions you think the author wants the reader to make about the situation.

Reinforce your skills

The skills of inference and deduction can also help build your understanding of a character in a novel or play. The extract below is the opening paragraph of Graham Greene's novel *Brighton Rock,* which is set in the 1930s with a gang war raging through the seaside town of Brighton.

1   As you read the text, use appropriate reading strategies to help you understand what is happening. What type of story do you think the novel will be? What are you told about the character of Hale? Discuss your ideas with a partner.

2   Look at how the character of Hale is described. Complete the table making inferences about Hale's character.

> **GLOSSARY**
>
> cynical – distrustful

Hale knew, before he had been in Brighton three hours, that they meant to murder him. With his inky fingers and his bitten nails, his manner cynical and nervous, anyone could tell he didn't belong – belong to the early summer sun, the cool Whitsun wind off the sea, the holiday crowd. They came in by train from Victoria every five minutes, rocked down Queen's Road standing on the tops of the little local trams, stepped off in bewildered multitudes into fresh and glittering air: the new silver paint sparkled on the piers, the cream houses ran away into the west like a pale Victorian watercolour; a race in miniature motors, a band playing, flower gardens in bloom below the front, an aeroplane advertising something for the health in pale vanishing clouds across the sky.

Details about Hale	What you can infer from these
'inky fingers'	• Involved with writing • Not interested in his appearance • Untidy? Dirty? • In a hurry?
'bitten nails'	
'his manner cynical'	
'nervous'	
'knew ... they meant to murder him'	
'anyone could tell he didn't belong'	

3 Look at the inferences you have made about Hale. Putting these together, what overall impression do you get about how Hale feels and his state of mind? Discuss your ideas with a partner.

4 Write a paragraph explaining what you have inferred about Hale's state of mind. You should include quotations from the extract and explain what you have inferred from these.

Support

When you infer, don't just repeat details from the text. Make sure that you interpret these details to make your own inferences, e.g.

'When the writer says Hale has 'bitten nails' this suggests that he bites his nails.' ✗

'When the writer says Hale has 'bitten nails' this makes it seem as though Hale is worried about something as this is something that you do when you are nervous.' ✓

Stretch

Try to develop a detailed exploration of how the character of Hale is built up. Look at how different details can be put together to suggest different meanings.

- Read the extract again, but this time ignore the first sentence. What would the details included about Hale suggest about his character if you didn't know he thought he was about to be murdered?

- Now reread the first sentence. What effect do the details here have on the inferences and deductions you make about Hale?

Extend your skills

You are now going to look at how you can use your skills of inference and deduction to build an impression of the mood or atmosphere in the text.

1   Reread the opening of *Brighton Rock* on page 83 and look at the way the setting is described. What inferences can you make from the details the writer includes? Use the three steps you practised in the **Build your skills** section to work out what mood or atmosphere these help to create. The first one has been done for you.

Details about setting	What mood or atmosphere is created
'Fresh and glittering air ...'	'Fresh' and 'glittering' make us think of things that are new, clean, unspoiled and beautiful, while the phrase 'glittering air' makes the reader feel that the sun is making everything sparkle.

2   Write a paragraph explaining what the overall mood and atmosphere of the setting is. You should include the evidence you have found from the extract and explain the inferences you have made.

You have now built up a picture of the character of Hale and the atmosphere of the holiday crowds in Brighton. Looking back at the different inferences you have made can help you to think about the overall effect of the text.

3   Look at the phrase 'anyone could tell he didn't belong'. Using the information you have gathered, write a paragraph explaining why you think Hale feels out of place and how the writer has helped you to understand this.

Stretch

Look at the inferences you have made about different details in the text and think about how you can connect these to help you to answer the question you have been asked.

Apply your learning

This is the opening of the novel *Private Peaceful* by Michael Morpurgo. Private Peaceful is Tommo Peaceful, a World War I British soldier stationed in France. In this extract, Tommo is writing in his journal as he sits waiting for something.

They've gone now, and I'm alone at last. I have the whole night ahead of me, and I won't waste a single moment of it. I shan't sleep it away. I won't dream it away either. I mustn't, because every moment of it will be far too precious.

I want to try to remember everything, just as it was, just as it happened. I've had nearly eighteen years of yesterdays and tomorrows, and tonight I must remember as many of them as I can. I want tonight to be long, as long as my life, not filled with fleeting dreams that rush me on towards dawn.

Tonight, more than any other night of my life, I want to feel alive.

Task

1. Look at the first sentence: 'They've gone now, and I'm alone at last.' Who do you think 'they' are? How do you think the narrator feels about them?

2. What can you tell about the narrator? Pick out details from the text and explain what inferences you can make about Tommo.

3. What does Tommo mean when he says the night ahead is 'precious'? What clues from the passage tell you this?

4. Why do you think Tommo wants to remember everything?

5. Look at the following quotation: 'not filled with fleeting dreams that rush me on towards dawn'. Why do you think the writer has chosen the words 'fleeting' and 'rush'?

6. How would you describe the mood of the passage?

7. What impression do you get of the situation Tommo is in? Refer to details from the text in your answer.

8. Rewrite Tommo's journal entry, adding in details that describe how Tommo feels. Try to link these to details already included in the text. You can use the starter below.

   They've gone now, and I'm so relieved to be alone at last …

Assess to Progress

Look back at the answers you gave in the previous section and use these to assess your progress. Rate yourself for each skill by deciding which number on the scale below best shows your skill level.

1	2	3	4	5	6	7

I find this difficult.   I'm getting there.   I'm good at this.

- I can use inference to explore layers of meaning.

  Self-check: I was able to work out what the situation might be by exploring the words and phrases in the text.

- I can make deductions based on evidence.

  Self-check: I was able to understand how Tommo was feeling, using evidence from the text.

- Using inference and deduction, I can explain possible meanings and interpretations.

  Self-check: I was able to put together the inferences I had made to help me rewrite Tommo's journal to include my inferences and deductions.

SKILLS FOR LIFE

Your school has sent a leaflet home to parents. It gives the following information about the NHS Direct National Helpline.

1 Look at the picture

a) What can you infer about how the mother is feeling?

b) What can you infer about how the girl is feeling?

2 Now read the text. How could NHS Direct help in this situation?

3 How does the text stress the importance of the helpline number?

4 The helpline has a 'dedicated team of nurses and advisors'. What does this mean?

"should I keep her off school?"

Available 24 hours NHS Direct

0845 46 47

The National Healthline

Next time you have any kind of question about health, call NHS Direct.

We have a dedicated team of nurses and advisors ready to give you all the help you need 24 hours a day.

Save this number and keep it safe in your purse or by the phone.

You'll also find help at www.nhsdirect.nhs.uk.

Progress in ... Analysing how texts are organised and structured

LEARNING OBJECTIVES

- Identify the different techniques used to organise ideas.
- Explain how layout and presentational choices can create different effects.
- Explain how different structural and organisational choices are used to create particular effects.

Activate your learning

Read the following extracts.

A The feather lay in my palm. I held it carefully, aware of its age and its fragility. Yet its whiteness was still translucent, the vermillion tips of the pinions still brilliant. ... I looked more closely at the feather. It lay across the scar on my right palm where I had burned my hand a long time ago ...

B The dome of the tower has long openings on every side. When the abbot reaches the top, Dracula is already standing at his favourite post, staring across the water, his hands clasped behind him in a characteristic gesture of thought, of planning. The abbot has seen him stand this way in front of his warriors, directing the strategy for the next day's raid.

C Now small fowls flew screaming over the yet yawning gulf; a sullen white surf beat against its steep sides; then all collapsed, and the great shroud of the sea rolled on as it rolled five thousand years ago.

D The nape of her neck, which had been so perfect, so white, was layered with scars of red and purple where her hair had burned her flesh. I placed my damaged hand over it, covering her scars with my own. We stood like that for a long time. I heard the harsh cry of the heron as it flew to its roost, the endless song of the water, and the quick beating of my heart.

E The story that follows is one I never intended to commit to paper. Recently, however, a shock of sorts has prompted me to look back over the most troubling episodes of my life and of the lives of the several people I loved best.

F Call me Ishmael. Some years ago – never mind how long precisely – having little or no money in my purse, and nothing particular to interest me on shore, I thought I would sail about a little and see the watery part of the world.

1 a) The six extracts are either the beginning or ending of three different novels. Working in pairs, discuss which extracts you think go together. Look for evidence from the extracts to help you to decide.

   b) Now decide which you think are openings and which you think are endings. Make a note of your reasons.

   c) Join with another pair and share the choices you have made. Did you make the same decisions?

2 Working in a group of four, make a list of five features you would expect in an opening and five things you expect in an ending to a novel. Use examples from the extracts to help you.

Assess to Progress

How good are you at explaining how texts are organised and presented? Copy the grid below, ticking the relevant box next to each skill. If you need help, think about things you have read recently.

I can ...	Easily	Sometimes	Not very often
Identify a range of techniques for organising ideas e.g. *When I'm reading a magazine article, I can spot how the opening tries to grab my attention.*			
Explain how layout and presentational choices create particular effects e.g. *When I read a leaflet, I can explain how bullet points are used to give information in a quick and easy-to-read way.*			
Explain how the way a text is structured creates a particular effect on the reader e.g. *When I am reading a novel, I can explain how the writer builds up to an unexpected ending.*			

Build your skills

The text below is taken from a leaflet encouraging visitors to Hack Green Nuclear Bunker, which was rebuilt in the 1980s as a shelter for the Regional Government should Britain have suffered a nuclear attack. Read the leaflet and answer the questions, thinking about the different **organisational and presentational features** used in the text and the **effects** these create.

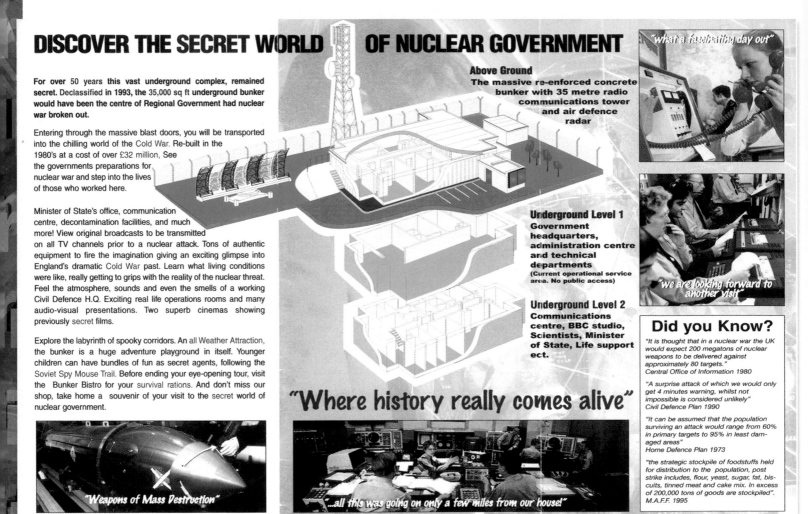

DISCOVER THE SECRET WORLD **OF NUCLEAR GOVERNMENT**

"what a fascinating day out"

For over 50 years this vast underground complex, remained secret. Declassified in 1993, the 35,000 sq ft underground bunker would have been the centre of Regional Government had nuclear war broken out.

Entering through the massive blast doors, you will be transported into the chilling world of the Cold War. Re-built in the 1980's at a cost of over £32 million, See the governments preparations for nuclear war and step into the lives of those who worked here.

Minister of State's office, communication centre, decontamination facilities, and much more! View original broadcasts to be transmitted on all TV channels prior to a nuclear attack. Tons of authentic equipment to fire the imagination giving an exciting glimpse into England's dramatic Cold War past. Learn what living conditions were like, really getting to grips with the reality of the nuclear threat. Feel the atmosphere, sounds and even the smells of a working Civil Defence H.Q. Exciting real life operations rooms and many audio-visual presentations. Two superb cinemas showing previously secret films.

Explore the labyrinth of spooky corridors. An all Weather Attraction, the bunker is a huge adventure playground in itself. Younger children can have bundles of fun as secret agents, following the Soviet Spy Mouse Trail. Before ending your eye-opening tour, visit the Bunker Bistro for your survival rations. And don't miss our shop, take home a souvenir of your visit to the secret world of nuclear government.

Above Ground
The massive re-enforced concrete bunker with 35 metre radio communications tower and air defence radar

Underground Level 1
Government headquarters, administration centre and technical departments
(Current operational service area. No public access)

Underground Level 2
Communications centre, BBC studio, Scientists, Minister of State, Life support ect.

"we are looking forward to another visit"

"Where history really comes alive"

"Weapons of Mass Destruction"

"...all this was going on only a few miles from our house!"

Did you Know?

"It is thought that in a nuclear war the UK would expect 200 megatons of nuclear weapons to be delivered against approximately 80 targets."
Central Office of Information 1980

"A surprise attack of which we would only get 4 minutes warning, whilst not impossible is considered unlikely"
Civil Defence Plan 1990

"It can be assumed that the population surviving an attack would range from 60% in primary targets to 95% in least damaged areas"
Home Defence Plan 1973

"the strategic stockpile of foodstuffs held for distribution to the population, post strike includes, flour, yeast, sugar, fat, biscuits, tinned meat and cake mix. In excess of 200,000 tons of goods are stockpiled".
M.A.F.F. 1995

1   Which three techniques does the main heading uses? Think about both the presentation and the use of language. Working with a partner, record each technique used and explain what effect it creates in a table like the one below. The first one has been done for you.

Technique	Effect created
Use of block capitals	This makes the main heading stand out more than the other text, which makes it seem more important.

Look again at the opening paragraph of the leaflet.

> For over 50 years this vast underground complex remained secret. Declassified in 1993, the 35,000 sq ft underground bunker would have been the centre of Regional Government had nuclear war broken out.

This writer has made the following presentational and structural choices:

- different colours for some words
- a smaller font than the main heading but a larger font than the rest of the leaflet
- a short paragraph.

2   Match each of the following explanations to the presentational features identified above.

a) They've done this because they want to make it short and easy to read. Too much information would be off-putting.

b) They've done this because it's less important than the main heading, but it makes the information in this paragraph stand out more.

c) They've done this because they wanted to make some words stand out.

When we look at the presentational and structural features used in a text, it is important to think about the **purpose** of the text and how these features help this purpose.

3   How do the presentational features used in the leaflet help the writer **inform** us about the bunker or **persuade** us to go there? Write a short paragraph and include comments on:

- the photographs included
- the quotations picked out
- the diagram.

Reinforce your skills

The extract opposite is taken from the opening of the novel *The Devil's Breath* by David Gilman.

1   As you read, think about the way the writer has organised the text. Then, working in pairs, discuss the following questions.

   a) What effect does the opening sentence have on you as a reader?

   b) Why do you think the writer began with a one-sentence paragraph?

   c) What questions does the second paragraph raise?

   d) What effect does the repetition used in the third paragraph have?

   e) How does the author link the final paragraphs back to the others?

It is important to develop your comments when explaining a writer's reasons for organising a text in a particular way and the effect this has. Halima has answered the first question about the opening of the story, but she hasn't developed her explanations.

2   Look at the organisational features Halima has identified and read her comments. Work with your partner to develop the explanations.

Organisational feature or structural choice	Halima's comment	Develop the explanation
The writer has used a single-sentence opening paragraph.	They've done this to make it more dramatic.	This technique works because it makes you stop and take a breath before the next paragraph and it makes it stand out, which suggests it's an important paragraph.
The writer has given us a description of the setting and background in the second paragraph.	They've done this so we can imagine it.	This technique works because ...
The writer has given us some suspicious events in the third paragraph.	They've done this to build up the suspense.	This technique works because ...

> ## Stretch
>
> What does the writer want the opening of the novel to do? Write a paragraph explaining how the structural choices help to create an effective opening for the novel. Refer to the different features used and the choices the writer has made and explain how they support his purpose.

The killer, like many assassins, came in the night.

The distant, echoing boom of gunfire and the lazy but deadly arc of machine guns' tracer rounds seeking out their target across windswept countryside would help to hide his presence. And tonight would be one of his easiest assignments. His victim was a fifteen-year-old boy, so he was in no doubt as to the success of his night's work.

He checked his watch. His timing was good. He was in position. First choice: make it look like an accident – a broken neck. Second choice: a shot to the head and dispose of the body. It made no difference to him. The wind had veered from the east to the north – there was a colder bite to it and he thought of the soldiers lying out there in the waterlogged ground. They would not have slept for days and, with the almost constant gunfire and the demands of patrolling, exhaustion and the cold would have eaten into them. Not him, though; his zipped roll-neck was mohair and his topcoat was a padded Timberland (no external Gore-Tex to make any rustling sound) and his Rockport boots were waterproof. It was good kit that kept his muscles warm and ready to move in that split second when speed and agility were needed.

Apply your learning

Task You are going to read two versions of Anthony Horowitz's novel *Stormbreaker.* The first is taken from the opening of the novel and the second is taken from the opening of the graphic novel version.

The first three questions are about the novel extract.

1 What do you notice about the way the paragraphs are organised?

   a) How are the paragraphs linked to one another? What do you notice about the order?

   b) Why has the writer organised the paragraphs in this way? What effect does each paragraph have on the reader?

2 How successful is this as an opening? Why do you think Anthony Horowitz has put this episode at the beginning of the novel? What effect does it have on the reader?

3 What clues are there that this is the first novel in the Alex Rider series?

The next two questions are about the graphic novel extract.

4 What do you notice about the panels and the way they are organised? What effect do these have on you as a reader? Think about:

   ● the size of the panels and the way they have been arranged

   ● the fonts used for speech bubbles and sound effects.

5 How successful is this as the opening of the graphic novel? Why do you think the writer and artist put this episode at the beginning of the novel? What effect does it have on the reader?

The last question is about both extracts.

6 The graphic novel begins with a cut from Alex to his uncle being chased, yet the novel only mentions a police car.

   a) What is the purpose of starting the novel in a less dramatic and more serious way? What effect does this have on the reader?

   b) What is the purpose of starting the graphic novel in a more dramatic way? What effect does this have on the reader?

When the doorbell rings at three in the morning, it's never good news.

Alex Rider was woken by the first chime. His eyes flickered open but for a moment he stayed completely still in his bed, lying on his back with his head resting on the pillow. He heard a bedroom door open and a creak of wood as somebody went downstairs. The bell rang a second time and he looked at the alarm clock glowing beside him. 3:02 a.m. There was a rattle as someone slid the security chain off the front door.

He rolled out of bed and walked over to the open window, his bare feet pressing down the carpet pile. The moonlight spilled on to his chest and shoulders. Alex was fourteen, already well-built, with the body of an athlete. His hair, cut short apart from two thick strands hanging over his forehead, was fair. His eyes were brown and serious. For a moment he stood silently, half-hidden in the shadow, looking out. There was a police car parked outside. From his second-floor window Alex could see the black ID number on the roof and the caps of the two men who were standing in front of the door. The porch light went on and, at the same time, the door opened.

'Mrs Rider?'

'No. I'm the housekeeper. What is it? What's happened?'

'This is the home of Mr Ian Rider?'

'Yes.'

'I wonder if we could come in...'

And Alex already knew.

1   a) Look at the examples on the previous page. Choose the three that you feel use language in the most effective or interesting way, for example language that is unexpected, dramatic, visual, surprising, playful or emotional.

    b) Compare your choices with a partner's. Discuss the examples you have chosen and try to work out what it is that makes them so effective. What techniques and language features has the writer used?

2   Choose one of the examples. Write a few sentences commenting on the language techniques it uses and the effects these create.

Assess to Progress

How good are you already at analysing a writer's choice of words and commenting on the effects that they create? Using the scale below, give yourself a rating for each of the following skills.

| 1 | 4 | 5 | 6 | 7 |

I find this difficult.　　　　I'm getting there.　　　　I'm good at this.

● I can recognise the techniques and language features that writers use to produce particular effects.

Self-check: Do you understand what different techniques, such as alliteration, onomatopoeia and metaphor, are and understand the effects they can create?

● I can explore the effects these techniques and features of language create.

Self-check: Can you explain how headlines use metaphor and comment on the effect this creates?

● I can recognise and comment on how a writer's language choices contribute to the overall effect on the reader.

Self-check: When you read advertisements, can you identify where the writers have used puns and word play to create a bigger impact and amuse the reader?

Language

Build your skills

Writers choose language to fit their purpose and provoke particular responses or influence their readers in certain ways. Read the descriptions of theme park attractions below and then use the skill steps to help you explore the way language is used.

The White Water River Rapids is a fast water ride. You might get wet.

White Water River Rapids

Swirl through rushing rapids, crash over waves, tear past rugged rocks and get ready for bumps, spray and a spectacular wall of water as you dare to ride the mighty white water. At the end of this ride, you may feel like a drowned rat but you will have had the time of your life! Can you dare not to?

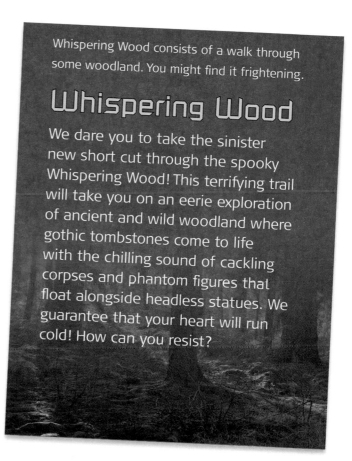

Whispering Wood consists of a walk through some woodland. You might find it frightening.

Whispering Wood

We dare you to take the sinister new short cut through the spooky Whispering Wood! This terrifying trail will take you on an eerie exploration of ancient and wild woodland where gothic tombstones come to life with the chilling sound of cackling corpses and phantom figures that float alongside headless statues. We guarantee that your heart will run cold! How can you resist?

Step 1 Identify key words, phrases and language features and begin to explore their effects

1   Look at the description of the White Water River Rapids ride. Discuss with a partner how the writer uses language to try to encourage people to experience the ride. Think about:

- The images created. Discuss the pictures you could see in your mind.

- Your first impression of the ride. Does it sound exciting and dangerous or boring?

- The language techniques the writer uses and their effect.

Let's look at the words and techniques that David has picked out.

I think the ride sounds like it is dangerous and exciting. The way the writer uses powerful action verbs like 'crash', 'tear' and 'swirl' and combines these with similarly powerful adjectives such as 'rushing rapids' and 'rugged rocks' gives me this impression.

The writer uses onomatopoeia when he writes about the way you 'crash' over waves. He also uses alliteration when he repeats the 's' sound in the words 'swirl', 'spray' and 'spectacular', which imitate the hissing sound of the water. Using these techniques brings the excitement of the ride to life.

2   Working with a partner, now read the description of the Whispering Wood attraction.

a)   What impression do you get of this attraction?

b)   Pick out the words and phrases that give you this impression. Look particularly at how **emotive language** is used (words that have been used to provoke an emotion).

c)   What language techniques does the writer use in this description? What effect does each technique create?

3   Write a short paragraph explaining your impression of the ride and picking out the words and phrases that helped to give this impression.

Step 2   Comment on the overall effect a writer's language choices and techniques create

It is important not just to spot different features and techniques, but to be able to talk about the overall effect that these create for the reader. To help you to do this, you need to look at the whole piece of writing and how the use of different techniques helps to build up an impression.

1   Look again at the description of the White Water River Rapids ride. You have already spotted the use of onomatopoeia, to emphasise the noise and power of the water, in the word 'crashed'.

a)   The word 'crashed' has other connotations too. **Connotation** means the suggested meanings or associations a word has. What does the word 'crash' make you think of?

b)   What impression do you get when you put the words 'crash', 'tear' and 'bumps' together?

c)   What is the overall impression created when the writer adds the phrase 'spectacular wall of water'? Think about how these different words and phrases are connected and the image they create.

Look at the way David has used a PEEL (Point – Evidence – Elaboration – Link) table to record his ideas.

Point	Evidence	Elaboration	Link
The writer makes the ride sound dangerous.	S/he uses onomatopoeic words such as 'crash' that make the ride sound like a dramatic accident such as a car crash.	The idea that the ride is out of control is taken further with the words 'tear' and 'bumps' which fit in with the idea of a car crash. When the writer then mentions a 'wall of water', the idea of crashing into this is at the front of the reader's mind.	The overall impact of choosing these words and phrases makes the reader feel like the ride will be nerve-racking and dangerous.

2 Look again at the description of the Whispering Wood. Using the skills you have been practising, explain the overall effect that the writer's use of language creates. Record your ideas in a PEEL table.

Support

Think about the connotations of the following words: 'eerie', 'spooky'. What do they make you think of? Pick out any words and techniques that add to this impression.

Stretch

What do you notice about the types and lengths of the sentences used in the description of the White Water River Rapids ride? How do these add to the overall effect the writer is trying to create?

Reinforce your skills

Writers can also use language to create powerful effects that bring a place alive for a reader. The following extract is from the author Jamila Gavin's autobiography *Out of India*, describing her childhood growing up in India. Here she writes about how important water is to the local people and to the land.

1   Read the text and think about how the emotive language used affects you as a reader. Look out for any words or ideas that the author repeats and think about the types and lengths of sentences she uses.

GLOSSARY

cataract – waterfall
carousel – a rotating stand
gullies – drainage ditches
irrigate – supply land with water
monsoon – rainy season

I see water held in the cup of a hand to drink, to rinse your mouth after teeth brushing and to wash the face and the arms. I see a long cataract of silver liquid pouring steadily and economically from a jug over the body and over the head. I see brown skin glistening with water. I see water belching out from the pump and the spray of water, like tossed diamonds, flung out of the watering can onto the dry flowerbeds. I see water glinting dark and dangerous at the bottom of a forty-foot deep well. I see water spewed out from a carousel of tin cans, tossing it out into gullies to irrigate the fields as the bullock or camel or buffalo treads its path round and round the well. And I see rainwater, sheeting down during monsoon and people rushing out with open mouths and outstretched arms, their clothes merging into their skins. Water is precious. Water is sacred.

Language

Working with a partner, answer the following questions about the text on the previous page. Use the skill steps you practised in the previous section.

2   What does the author compare water with in the second sentence? Why do you think she has chosen this metaphor?

3   Pick out examples of powerful verbs the writer includes in the passage. Describe the effect of each example.

4   a) What words and phrases does the writer repeat through the passage?

   b) Why do you think she does this? What effect does this have on you as a reader?

5   Why do you think the author finishes the paragraph with two very short sentences? What does it add to the way she wants you to feel about water?

6   Write a paragraph explaining how the writer uses language to make us understand that water is important in this text.

Support

You could use some of the following sentence starters to help you organise your explanation:

- By using the word ... the author is suggesting that ...
- The writer uses ... By using this technique she seems to be ...
- ... is a word that will make the reader take note because ...
- When the author uses ... it makes the reader feel that ...

Don't forget to use quotation marks when you are including quotations from the text in your explanation.

Stretch

Explore the word choices and techniques used across the whole passage and show how these link together to develop the overall effect on the reader.

- Water is described in many different ways in the passage, such as ...
- This creates the impression that ...
- By the end of the paragraph, the reader is left feeling that ...

Extend your skills

You are now going to read another piece of writing about water. This is a poem called 'Rain on Dry Ground' by Christopher Fry, which describes a sudden downpour on a dry, parched meadow.

1 Working with a partner, take it in turns to read the poem aloud. What first impression do you get from it?

> That is rain on dry ground. We heard it;
> We saw the little tempest in the grass,
> The panic of anticipation: heard
> The uneasy leaves flutter, the air pass
> In a wave, the fluster of the vegetation;
>
> Heard the first spatter of drops, the outriders
> Larruping on the road, hitting against
> The gate of the drought, and shattering
> Onto the lances of the tottering meadow.
> It is rain; it is rain on dry ground.
>
> Rain riding suddenly out of the air,
> Battering the bare walls of the sun.
> It is falling on to the tongue of the blackbird,
> Into the heart of the thrush; the dazed valley
> Sings it down. Rain, rain on dry ground! …
>
> The rain stops.
> The air is sprung with green.
> The intercepted drops
> Fall at their leisure; and between
> The threading runnels on the slopes
> The snail drags his caution into the sun.

GLOSSARY

outriders – people who ride in front of someone or something important

larruping – aggressively beating

lances – thin poles with sharp points used as weapons by soldiers on horseback

runnels – narrow channels of running water

2 a) Discuss with your partner what type of language features you might normally expect to find in a poem, e.g. rhyme, rhythm, word patterns.

   b) Look again at the poem you have just read. Can you find any of these features or techniques?

   c) For each feature you identify, comment on the effect you think it creates. Compare your answer with your partner's.

3 The writer of this poem uses **personification**, where non-human things are given human qualities: the grass 'anticipates', the leaves are 'uneasy', the vegetation is 'flustered' when it starts to rain.

   a) Why do you think the writer uses this technique? What effect does it create?

   b) Look at how he personifies the first raindrops as 'outriders'. What does he describe them as doing? How does this add to the overall effect he creates?

4 Why do you think the last stanza is set out differently? Look at what it describes and how this is different from what has gone before.

5 Working with a partner, prepare another reading of the poem. One of you should read the poem but stop at the end of each stanza. The other person should then give the 'director's commentary' on the stanza explaining how the writer has created deliberate effects with his choices of language and techniques.

Apply your learning

Task Working on your own, read the leaflet on the following page from the housing and homelessness charity Shelter and then complete the activities that follow. Remember to use the skills and techniques you have developed through this unit to help you complete the activities.

1 Reread the introductory paragraph. Which words or phrases persuade the reader that there is a problem? What effect do you think they have on the reader? Copy and complete the table below.

Words and phrases	How they persuade the reader there is a problem	What effect they have on the reader

Language

Shelter's million children campaign

It's shocking that, in one of the richest countries in the world, more than one million children live in housing that is overcrowded, run-down, damp, or dangerous. Some live in housing that's making them ill. Many are missing out on a decent education. Others suffer chronic insecurity, shuffled from place to place in so-called 'temporary' accommodation. They deserve better.

In twenty-first century England, how can this happen?

There simply aren't enough decent, affordable homes. While families wait for years at the bottom of council housing waiting lists in overcrowded areas, elsewhere dilapidated homes lie empty. Dangerous, neglected estates become no-go areas. And second home ownership is pricing local people out of many rural areas.

Children are paying the price. In 2004 Shelter launched its million children campaign to wake people up to the shocking scale and reality of the housing crisis, and to help end bad housing for the next generation.

2 'They deserve better.' Why do you think the introductory paragraph ends with this very short sentence?

3 Choose the statement that you think best describes how the writer of this leaflet wants the reader to feel. Support your choice with evidence from the text.

a) Angry that children may miss out on their education.

b) Sympathetic towards children who are living in difficult circumstances.

c) Shocked at the conditions some children live in.

4 Look at the following quotations taken from the leaflet. For each one explain what effect you think the words and phrases in **bold** would have on a parent reading them.

- 'children live in housing that is overcrowded, **run-down, damp, or dangerous**'

- '**Some** live in housing that's making them ill. **Many** are missing out ... **Others** suffer chronic insecurity'

- '**In twenty-first century England, how can this happen?**'

5 Pick out any powerful adjectives that the writer uses. What effects does the writer create by using these adjectives?

6 Which examples of the writer using emotive language do you think are the most powerful? Explain why you have chosen them.

Assess to Progress

How good are you now at analysing a writer's choice of words and commenting on the effects that they create? Look back at the ratings you gave yourself on page 101 and decide whether any of them should change. Use the work you have done in this unit to help you make your decisions.

| 1 | 3 | 4 | 5 | 6 | 7 |

I find this difficult.   I'm getting there.   I'm good at this.

- I can recognise the techniques and language features that writers use to produce particular effects.

- I can explore the effects these techniques and features of language create.

- I can recognise and comment on how a writer's language choices contribute to the overall effect on the reader.

Your mum is looking for a present for your young cousin. He is nine years old and his hobby is birdwatching. She has found this gift for sale on the RSPB website, but wants your advice as to whether it is suitable for your cousin.

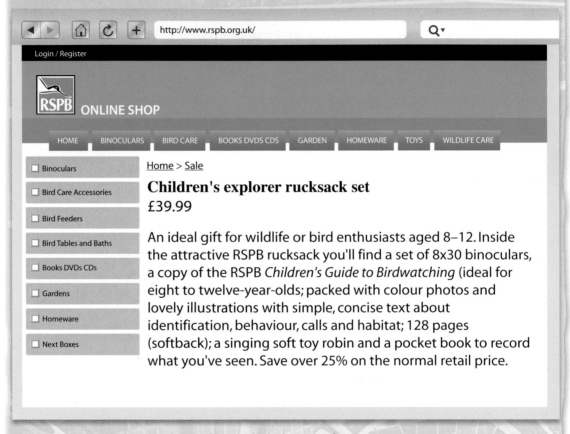

http://www.rspb.org.uk/

Login / Register

RSPB ONLINE SHOP

HOME | BINOCULARS | BIRD CARE | BOOKS DVDS CDS | GARDEN | HOMEWARE | TOYS | WILDLIFE CARE

- Binoculars
- Bird Care Accessories
- Bird Feeders
- Bird Tables and Baths
- Books DVDs CDs
- Gardens
- Homeware
- Next Boxes

Home > Sale

Children's explorer rucksack set

£39.99

An ideal gift for wildlife or bird enthusiasts aged 8–12. Inside the attractive RSPB rucksack you'll find a set of 8x30 binoculars, a copy of the RSPB *Children's Guide to Birdwatching* (ideal for eight to twelve-year-olds; packed with colour photos and lovely illustrations with simple, concise text about identification, behaviour, calls and habitat; 128 pages (softback); a singing soft toy robin and a pocket book to record what you've seen. Save over 25% on the normal retail price.

1. How many items does the rucksack contains?

2. Which of the following words make the product sound appealing?

   - concise • attractive • packed

3. How does the advert impress upon the reader that the product is good value for money?

4. Explain whether you think this is a good present for your cousin. Pick out any words and phrases that helped you decide.

Progress in ... Understanding and responding to ideas, viewpoints, themes and purposes in texts

LEARNING OBJECTIVES ★

- Trace the development of a writer's ideas and viewpoints and track how themes are developed.
- Respond to a text by making precise points and providing relevant evidence in support of your points.
- Explain how ideas, themes or characters can have an effect on the reader.

Activate your learning

The 'Mosquito' is a device which emits a high-pitched sound that can only be heard by young people and is used to deter them from hanging around in certain places. Read the following two press releases about the 'Mosquito'.

Text A
ACS defends Mosquito device

The Association of Convenience Stores has waded into the row over the use of high-frequency 'Mosquito' devices to disperse gangs of youths gathering outside shops.

ACS chief executive James Lowman defended use of the devices, saying: 'Unfortunately in many locations around the country retailers are victims of anti-social gangs of youths that congregate around their premises.'

'These youths deter customers, intimidate staff and can commit vandalism and violence. Where a retailer is faced with this problem we fully support the use of a Mosquito device sparingly and as a measure of last resort.'

Text B
Ultrasonic dispersal devices told to BUZZ OFF

Makers and users of ultrasonic dispersal devices, referred to as 'Mosquitoes', are being challenged by campaigners who say the device is discriminatory against young people.

The national campaign, BUZZ OFF, is spearheaded by young people and has been launched to raise awareness of the devices. The campaign is being supported by the Children's Commissioner for England, Liberty, Groundwork and the National Youth Agency.

Showing his support, Sir Al Aynsley-Green, Children's Commissioner for England, said: 'I have spoken to many children and young people from all over England who have been deeply affected by ultrasonic teenage deterrents. These devices are indiscriminate and target ALL children and young people, including babies, regardless of whether they are behaving or misbehaving.'

1   Working with a partner, discuss what viewpoint each text presents about the 'Mosquito' device.

2   For each text, write a sentence summarising the writer's viewpoint. Pick out any details from the text that helped you to decide on the viewpoint.

3   Choose one quotation from each article that best shows the main idea in the text. Discuss your choice with a partner.

4   Which press release would the photo best accompany? Discuss your decision with a partner, thinking about the effect the image will have on a reader.

Assess to Progress

How good are you already at understanding and responding to the ideas and viewpoints in different texts? How good are you at identifying the theme and purpose of a text? Rate yourself for each skill by deciding which number on the scale below best shows your skill level. You will need to be able to justify your decisions, so try to think of examples that support your choice.

| 1 | | 3 | 4 | 5 | 6 | 7 |

I find this difficult.   I'm getting there.   I'm good at this.

● I can trace the development of writers' ideas and work out a writer's viewpoint.

   Self-check: Could you work out how the writer of each text felt about the 'Mosquito'? How many details did you pick out from the text that showed this?

● I can make precise points and use relevant evidence to support my points.

   Self-check: Could you write a sentence summing up the main idea in each text? Did you back this up with a helpful quotation?

● I am aware of the impact of texts on readers and I can explain it.

   Self-check: How well did you explain the reasons for pairing the photo with a press release? Did you think about what effect the photo would have on the reader?

Build your skills

Being able to trace a writer's ideas and viewpoint in a text allows you to understand how an argument is built and how themes are developed. Use the skill steps below to help you trace the main ideas and viewpoint in the following newspaper article. Explore the effect they have on the reader.

Step 1 ## Work out the main ideas, identifying purpose and viewpoint and how they develop

Headlines often give you an overview of what articles are about (the **main idea**), but can also suggest what the writers think (the **viewpoint**) and (their **purpose**).

1 Working with a partner, read the newspaper report and then discuss the questions around the text.

Too much testing harms primary school pupils

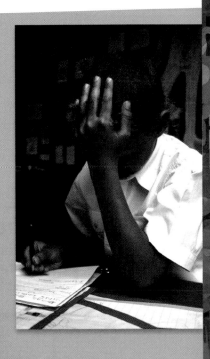

a) How does this tell us that the report will be about how young children are tested too often?

The repeated testing of young children is seriously undermining their education, a major study reports.

b) How do the words 'anxiety' and 'stress' develop the writer's viewpoint?

Hours spent drilling pupils increases 'anxiety and stress', narrows the curriculum and has limited impact on standards, it is claimed.

e) What picture does this give about what the writer thinks is happening in schools?

Children aged 11 spend almost three weeks practising and sitting tests in their final year of primary school in England – while teachers waste five weeks preparing exams.

d) What do the words 'waste' and 'wasted' suggest the writer's viewpoint is?

Despite claims that children are brighter than ever, researchers said the system of high-stakes tests had 'exaggerated' pupils' progress, with up to a third given the wrong grades. In a damning conclusion, the report says £500 million spent on Labour's National Literacy Strategy had been wasted as children's ability to read was no better than in the 1950s.

e) What idea does the writer end the article with? What does this suggest about his viewpoint?

Reinforce your skills

You are now going to look at how you can trace a writer's ideas and themes in a fiction text. The extract is from the opening of *The Wind Singer,* a fantasy novel by William Nicholson about a world where everybody is tested. Read the extract and with a partner, answer the questions opposite.

Today was the day of Pinpin's first test. She was only two years old, too little to mind how well or badly she did, but from now till the day she died she would have a rating. That was what was making him sad.

Tears started to push into Bowman's eyes. He cried too easily, everyone told him so, but what was he to do? He felt everything too much. He didn't mean to, but when he looked at somebody else, anybody else, he found he knew what they were feeling, and all too often it was a fear or a sadness. And then he would understand what it was they were afraid of or sad about, and he would feel it too, and he would start to cry. It was all very awkward.

This morning what made him sad wasn't what Pinpin was feeling now, but what he knew she would feel one day. Now there were no worries in her sunny little heart.
Yet from today, she would begin, at first only dimly, but later with a sharp anxiety, to fear the future. For in Aramanth, life was measured out in tests. Every test brought with it the possibility of failure, and every test successfully passed led to the next, with its renewed possibility of failure. There was no escape from it, and no end.

1 How does the writer show how Bowman feels about the tests that everybody has to take? Think about the words and phrases that best show:

  ● how Bowman feels about his sister Pinpin's first test

  ● how Bowman feels about the effects that the tests have on people.

2 a) What is the writer trying to get readers to think about? Can you find relevant evidence from the text to show this?

   b) What do you think the writer's viewpoint about testing is? Can you find a word or phrase that backs this point up?

3 Choose one theme from the list below and explain how the writer has developed this theme in the text.

  ● growing up

  ● feeling like a failure

  ● protecting children.

Stretch

Compare this extract with the newspaper report *Too much testing harms primary school pupils* on page 113. Working with a partner, discuss:

• what the main ideas in each text are and how they are developed by each writer.

• how the two writers' viewpoints are similar and how they are different.

• which text you think has the most impact on you as a reader and why.

Remember to make precise points and select relevant evidence to support these.

Extend your skills

When you are tracing a writer's viewpoint in a text, you need to be able to work out how the writer's attitude is suggested when it isn't made explicit. The text on the next page is from an interview with Corporal Clifford Lane who fought in World War I.

1 Read the text and then answer the questions around it to help you work out what Corporal Lane's attitude to the war was.

Task **Apply your learning**

Use the skills you have developed in this unit to answer the questions about the texts opposite, written by soldiers fighting in wars. Remember to make precise points and support these with relevant evidence.

These questions are about the first text, written by a British soldier in World War I.

1 Read the diary entry. Which of the following statements best describes Charlie Francis' point of view about being a Lance-Corporal? Explain why.

   a) He wants to be a Private instead.

   b) He is proud to be a Lance-Corporal.

   c) He doesn't care what rank he is – he is just pleased to be in the army.

2 How does Charlie's viewpoint change in his letters home? What does he think now about life in the military?

3 '... the infantry are just the targets.' What does this suggest about the writer's attitude to war?

These questions are about the second text, written by an American soldier in the Vietnam War.

4 Which of the following statements best describes Dean Allen's point of view about being a platoon leader? Explain why.

   a) He can't let himself get close to his men.

   b) He doesn't like his men.

   c) He likes being in charge of his men.

5 How does Dean Allen show his attitude to the war in the letter? Pick out three quotations from the text that help show this and explain these.

The last question is about both extracts.

6 Comment on how reading both texts made you feel about war. Select relevant evidence from both texts to support your points.

Private Charlie Ross Francis joined up in October 1915. In January 1917 he lost his Lance-Corporal's stripes and was demoted to the rank of Private for not reporting three men as drunk while he was on watch.

1 January 1916 (diary)
Beginning of a New Year in Military Life. Stationed at the Broadway Drill Hall, Winnipeg. I hold the rank of Provisional Lance-Corporal at this date and hope for further promotion in the near future. I am fairly comfortably quartered as I sleep in the sergeants' mess. Have a mattress, a pillow and two heavy blankets.

6 May 1917 (letter to his mother)
You mentioned one time that you hoped I'd get my stripes back again soon. Please don't wish anything like that on me for I am far better here as a private than a corporal with the battalion. The corporal who took my place was killed ...

21 June 1917 (letter to his sister Etta)
It may seem strange but in spite of the fact that I spent about seven months in the trenches I haven't shot off my rifle yet. That's modern warfare. The artillery do it all, or nearly all, the infantry are just the targets.

> ## GLOSSARY
>
> **artillery** – heavy weapons such as tanks
> **infantry** – soldiers with hand-held weapons
> **platoon** – band of soldiers

Excerpts of a letter from Lieutenant Dean Allen to his wife, Joyce

Dearest Wife,

I am out on ambush with eleven men and a medic – after everything is set up in position I have nothing to do but think about why I am here. Why do I have to be the one to tell someone to do something that may get him blown away?

Being a good platoon leader is a lonely job. I don't want to really get to know anybody over here because it would be bad enough to lose a man – I damn sure don't want to lose a friend. But as hard as I try not to get involved with my men I still can't help liking them, and getting close to a few. They come up and say 'Hey do you want to see picture of my wife or girl?'

Like I said it gets lonely trying to stay separate.

Maybe sometime I'll try to tell you how scared I am now. There is nothing I can do about it, but wait for another day to start and finish.

All my love always,

Dean

11:15

This 12-year-old boy has been complaining of toothache so his mum has taken him to the dentist. However, they were also doing a bit of shopping in the market. Ian and Andrea explain that the child should be returned to school as quickly as possible. His mum promises to take him straight back.

11:27

Andrea finishes off her records, while Ian contacts a school to check that a pupil they stopped earlier with his dad has been returned to school.

10:34

This 10-year-old girl is on holiday from the Republic of Ireland with her family visiting her gran. In this situation, Andrea still has to take a record of their details. But because the child comes from a foreign country, it is unlikely that anything will be done.

10:48

This 14-year-old has been permanently excluded and is due to go to a pupil referral unit. The school will be contacted to confirm the details, and arrangements will then be made to ensure he gets any necessary support.

Extend your learning

1   Reread the texts on pages 137 and 139-140. Work with a partner to compare them, recording the information in a table like the one below. Some details have been completed for you with questions to help you explore the different features.

	Truancy sweeps (page 137)	**On the truancy beat (pages 140)**
Purpose		To recount what happens on a truancy sweep. *Do you think it has any other purposes?*
Audience	Educated readers with an interest in truancy. *Who **in particular** might read this?*	
Organisation		Pictures with captions – like a storyboard. *How is the information in the captions organised?* Chronological order – with time sequence clearly visible.
Language	**Formal**: 'this power will be enacted'. *What other examples can you find?* **Serious and strong:** 'join forces'. *Find some other examples.* **Technical terms**: 'unauthorised absence'. **Impersonal**: facts and figures.	*Look at the sorts of words the writer chooses. For example, comment on how the writer uses nouns and adjectives. Remember to include some examples.*
Verbs and tenses	Mainly present tense to describe the current situation. Past tense to explain previous actions and research findings. Future tense to explain what will happen. Some passive: 'will be enacted' to add to the impersonal formality.	
Text type		

My child has been truanting/excluded and the school/LEA has offered a parenting contract — what happens now?
The school or LEA should invite you to a meeting to discuss the parenting contract. Your child may also be invited to attend, depending on their age and understanding.

- DO NOT WORRY. Parenting contracts are not a punishment and being offered a contract is not a bad reflection on you in any way.
- The meeting is for you and the school/LEA to discuss your child's attendance or behaviour, the reasons behind it and ways in which it might be improved. You can also use it to discuss more generally any difficulties which you/your family are having and types of support that may be helpful to you.
- The offer of a parenting contract is an opportunity for you and the school or LEA to work together to tackle any difficulties which your child is having. Tackling these issues now can make a real difference to your child's life chances. Repeated exclusions are very disruptive to a child's education and those who are excluded or who truant are far less likely than their peers to get five or more good GCSEs and more likely to become involved in crime.
- A parenting contract is also an opportunity for you to get help that you might need, both in relation to parenting and more generally.
- If you are anxious about the meeting, ask the school or LEA if you can bring a friend or family member along for moral support.

Questions 1 and 2 are about the text *On the truancy beat*.

1 Find the two cases where no action by the education welfare officer is necessary. Write down a brief quotation from the text to show each of the two cases you are identifying and then explain in your own words why no action will be taken.

2 Write down two skills that you think Ian and Andrea need in their jobs. Explain why you think this.

Question 3 to 5 are about the text *Parenting Contracts*.

3 Reread the opening section on page 143 from 'Every mum, dad and carer' to 'through a parenting contract'. Pick a word or group of words that suggest to the parent that a parenting contract is meant to HELP, not to PUNISH. Explain your choice. One example has been provided.

'if their child is having problems'	These words do not blame anybody for the child's problems. The words 'having problems' suggest that this may be something that happens from time to time.

4 Reread the third bullet point on page 143 begining 'Parenting contracts are NOT a punishment'. How does the writer expect parents to react to being given a parenting contract and how do you know?

5 Look at these two examples of the way the writer uses language. They are taken from the final section of the text. What effect do you think the words in **bold type** will have on a parent who reads them.

- Tackling these issues now **can make a real difference to your child's life chances**

- A parenting contract is also **an opportunity for you** to get help that **you might need**

Questions 6 and 7 are about the layout and organisation of both texts.

6 Copy and complete the grid comparing the layout and organisation of both texts. One example from each has been given.

On the truancy beat	Parenting Contracts
Example 1: There is a **sub-headline** – 'Ever wondered ...' This helps the reader because ... it makes it clear what the article is about and tells us the name of the reporter. The question raises the reader's interest.	Example 1: Some words are written in **capital letters**, e.g. 'DO NOT WORRY'. This helps the reader because ... it emphasises important words so that the reader notices them.
Example 2: This helps the reader because ...	Example 2: This helps the reader because ...
Example 3:	Example 3:

7 This question is about the **purpose** of the two texts, *On the truancy beat* and *Parenting Contracts*, and **the way they achieve their purpose**. Choose one statement for each text and then explain in your own words why you have chosen it.

	On the truancy beat
A	This text seeks to persuade young people that they should not truant from school. It does this by showing them how much trouble they will be in if they are caught on a truancy sweep.
B	This text seeks to inform people about what happens on a truancy sweep. It does this by providing a number of situations in which young people are questioned on a truancy sweep.

	Parenting Contracts
C	This text seeks to support parents whose children may be having problems at school. It does this by reassuring parents and involving them in the solution to their child's difficulties.
D	This text seeks to punish parents who do not take responsibility for their children. It does this by telling them exactly what will happen if they don't cooperate.

Assess to Progress

1 Which questions did you feel most confident about answering? Which questions did you feel less confident about?

2 Think about the different reading skills you have used in this unit. Rate yourself for each of the following skills by deciding which number on the scale below best shows your skill level.

- skimming and scanning to retrieve information
- inference and deduction
- paying close attention to language and organisation.

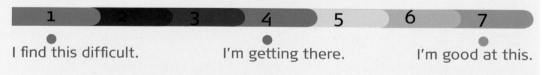

| 1 | 2 | 3 | 4 | 5 | 6 | 7 |

I find this difficult.   I'm getting there.   I'm good at this.

Progress in ...
Writing

Writing AF1
Progress in ... Generating ideas, planning and drafting

Activate your learning

Look at the storyboard below. This shows the opening of a spy thriller film.

1 a) Working in a group of four, discuss what might be happening in the scenes shown in the storyboard.

b) How could you turn the opening of this film into the start of a novel? Make notes on how you could describe these scenes from each of these different viewpoints:

a) I was relaxed and happy, the holidays were about to begin ...

b) I could not believe the danger of landing there ...

c) We were tense and nervous. It was essential we were not seen ...

d) He could have wrecked all our plans, I had to act ...

2 Choose one of the viewpoints from which to tell the story. Which planning format do you think would be the best to help you plan your writing? In your group, discuss the advantages and disadvantages of the following approaches.

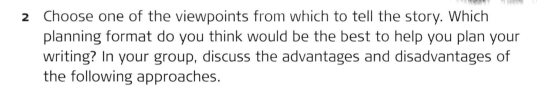

mind map   spidergram   chronology   bullets   timeline   headings

Assess to Progress

How good are you at drawing on the information you have been given to plan effectively? Do you find it easy to explore and develop ideas to suit the purpose of your writing? How good are you at creating an effective voice in your writing and developing characters and settings?

Rate yourself for each of the skills below. Give reasons for your answers based on writing you have recently completed.

1	2	3	4	5	6	7

I find this difficult.   I'm getting there.   I'm good at this.

- I can select and shape ideas to suit my purpose, adapting familiar forms and conventions.

- I can explore and connect ideas and choose the best way to plan my writing.

- I can produce thoughtful and imaginative texts to engage the reader.

Build your skills

In this unit you are going to explore how to develop ideas so that you can plan and craft your writing to meet the needs of your readers.

You are part of a team organising a mountain climbing holiday for teenagers. You have been asked to write an information sheet giving advice about the equipment to take, how to avoid danger when climbing and tips for survival at high altitudes.

Follow the skill steps below to help you plan and develop this writing.

Step 1 Select and shape the ideas you are given and develop these with your own

When you are given a task, **select** the words that help you to understand the audience and purpose for your writing, e.g.

teenagers	equipment	high altitudes	advice	dangers	survival

1 Now **shape** these into ideas you can use in your writing by developing and extending these words.

teenagers – group of active and adventurous youngsters ...

equipment – survival kit containing everything you need ...

high altitudes – mountain peaks ...

advice – helpful hints ...

dangers –

survival –

2 Can you think of any other ideas that you could include? Think about the **purpose** of your writing (to advise) and the **audience** you are writing for (teenagers).

Step 2 Use what you know to help you adapt familiar forms and conventions

It can be helpful to look at texts that have similar purposes or are written for the same audience and think about how you can adapt the techniques these use for your own writing. The text opposite is from the Mountain Rescue website – it has a similar purpose but is aimed at a wider audience.

http://www.mountain.rescue.org.uk/advice.php

Saving lives in wild and remote places

Home>

Search For

MRC Mountain Advice

British mountains can be killers without proper care. The following points cover the minimum precautions you should take if you want to avoid getting hurt or lost or, in the event of an accident, minimise further harm.

Equipment and its use

A map, compass (and the ability to use them), and at least one reliable watch in the party should always be carried.
If you carry a GPS, at least know how to read your current position.
It could save a lot of hassle in an emergency when speaking to the Mountain Rescue Team.
In all conditions, it is wise to carry a whistle, torch, spare batteries and bulbs;
but in winter conditions, an ice-axe, crampons and survival bag are essential.
Climbers and mountain bikers are all urged to wear helmets at all times.

Dangers – all can be avoided

Precipices
Slopes of ice or steep snow and grass slopes, especially if frozen or wet
Unstable boulders
Gullies, gorges, stream beds and streams in spate

Snow cornices on ridges or gully tops
Exceeding your experience and abilities
Loss of concentration, especially toward the end of a long day

Dangers – require constant monitoring

Weather changes – these can be sudden and more extreme than forecast
Ice on path (carry an ice-axe and crampons – and know how to use them)
Excessive cold or heat (dress appropriately)
Incipient exhaustion (know the signs; rest and keep warm)

Accident or illness (don't panic – if you send for help, make sure you stay put and the rescuers know exactly where to come)
Passage of time – especially true when under pressure – allow extra time in winter conditions

Pride

It is no disgrace to turn back if you are not certain. A party must be governed by the capabilities of the weakest member.

---

1   Use the following strategies to help you adapt the ideas and features in the Mountain Rescue text for use in your own writing.

- **Explore:** What are the main similarities and differences between this text and the text you need to write,
  e.g. Similarities – it stresses the serious dangers to be avoided.
       Differences – a teenage audience requires an informal approach.

- **Problem-solve:** Which ideas and features could you use in your own writing? How should you adapt them to suit your purpose and audience?

- **Connect:** How can you combine the ideas and features you have decided to adapt with your own ideas,
  e.g. The Mountain Rescue website tells you to dress appropriately.
  I could include some examples of appropriate clothing in the Equipment section of my information sheet.

GLOSSARY

incipient – early stages of
crampons – spikes on a boot to prevent slipping

Step 3 Choose the most appropriate approach to plan your writing

Which planning format do you think would be most helpful when planning and organising this type of writing? Think about the way the text you have just read was organised.

1. a) Select an appropriate planning format for your information sheet. Think about the planning formats listed on page 149 or any other planning formats you have used.

   b) Create your plan, keeping the purpose and audience for your writing in mind as you plan.

Step 4 Develop relevant material imaginatively

As you work on your plan, you need to think about the way you could **develop your ideas** in your writing. Think about the different techniques you could use to appeal to your readers. Look at the words used at the start of the Mountain Rescue text you have read:

'Mountains can be killers'

The writer uses personification to emphasise the danger of mountains.

1. Think of ways you could use similar techniques in your own writing.

   e.g. The summit could turn into an assassin if you're not prepared.

   Add these ideas to your plan in the sections where you think they will work best.

2. Use your plan to help you to draft your information sheet. When you have finished, compare your draft and plan with a partner and discuss the choices you made.

Reinforce your skills

You are now going to use the skill steps you have practised to help you to plan and develop a piece of fiction writing. You have been asked to adapt and develop a James Bond comic strip into a story to be read aloud. Read the extract below and work through the questions to help you to continue the story and write the next episode.

1   Working with a partner, work out what is happening in this episode,

e.g. James Bond is being chased by his enemies, when he is caught in an avalanche. Bond survives but ...

Language

2   Join with another pair, and look at the detail and information given in the comic strip. Think about the ideas you will adapt and develop in your story, thinking about:

- the purpose of your writing

- your audience – and their expectations

- what might happen next in the story.

3   Look again at the comic strip and think about how you can adapt the conventions it uses to help make sure you include the right ingredients in your story. Think about:

- turning the captions into pacey descriptions of setting and action

- developing a paragraph for each frame to structure events into an exciting plot

- how to create interesting characters, adding details of their thoughts and feelings

- including dramatic dialogue.

Support

Think about the ways you could develop your ideas in your writing. For example:

Using **comparisons** to make your writing dramatic:

'the great high snout of the avalanche was majestically pouring through the trees'

Including **similes and metaphors** to make the action more interesting:

'crouching over his ski-stick like a jouster's lance'

Extend your skills

When writing fiction or non-fiction, it is important to find the right **voice** to fit your writing. In stories, an author creates a narrative voice – the person telling the story. This could be:

- the voice of a character within the story. This is called a **first person narrative voice** and uses 'I' or 'we' to tell the story.

- a voice that isn't one of the characters in the story, but describes the events. This is called a **third person narrative voice** and use 'he', 'she' or 'they' to tell the story. Third person narratives can be **all-knowing** where the narrator can move around freely and describe the thoughts of different characters or **limited** where the narrator can only reveal the thoughts of one character.

1 Read the following reasons for choosing different narrative voices. Working with a partner, decide which apply to first person narratives and which apply to third person narratives. Which are advantages and which are disadvantages? Which have been applied in the text you have just read?

- Helps the reader relate to the person telling the story.

- Lets you tell the story from more than one viewpoint.

- Can only show the thoughts of the narrator.

- Can make the reader feel more distant from the main character.

Read the extract from the novel *Silverfin* by Charlie Higson below. The novel describes the adventures of the young James Bond.

For a long while he didn't move; he just lay there, face down, on a dusty, threadbare rug, breathing heavily. He felt sick. His head was pounding and sweat was pouring off him, stinging his eyes.

Then it slowly dawned on him that, in fact, he was far from safe, he was in a more dangerous position than before.

Jack was inside the giant's castle.

What was he going to do? Without Kelly he was lost. Their whole plan was shot to pieces. He knew nothing about creeping about houses in the middle of the night. Yes, he was in all right, but somehow he had to get out again. He couldn't go back the way he had come. He had to find some other exit from the castle, and he had to find it without waking anybody.

2   Working with a partner, read the extract and pick out the ways the narrative voice helps the reader understand James' feelings and emotions. Look at:

●   the words chosen to describe the action and setting

●   the way the character's thoughts are described.

3   a)   Look back at your plan you created for the story on page 154 . Try writing the opening sentences from a first person perspective and then from a third person perspective. Decide which type of narrative voice you will use to tell the story.

   b)   Draft your story. Make notes about how you will create the right voices in your script. Think about how you will show the difference between the voice of the narrator and the voice of the character. How will each of them sound?

Stretch

Think about the ways you can maintain the narrative voice you create in your story.
• Look at all the dialogue you have written for your main character and ask a partner to comment on whether this sounds like it is the same person speaking.
• Have you created a convincing narrative voice? Have you used a range of techniques to maintain this?

Apply your learning

Task   Working on your own, you are now going to use the skills you have developed in this unit to help you to write the opening to a chapter in a spy thriller called *The Slippery Slope*. This spy thriller is aimed at readers who are fans of books such as the Alex Rider and the Young Bond series.

At the end of the last chapter enemies have captured the hero, who is a spy.

1   Plan your writing. Use the skill steps to help you choose the most appropriate planning format. Think about how you can:

●   select and shape the ideas you have been given

●   develop and extend your own ideas

●   use what you know about this type of writing

●   create the right voice for your narrator

●   develop ideas for creating imaginative characters and setting.

2 Use your plan to draft the opening of the chapter. Keep the purpose and audience for your writing in mind and try to use different techniques to engage your readers.

Assess to Progress

How good are you now at generating ideas, planning and drafting? Look back at the ratings you gave yourself on page 149 and decide whether any of these should change. Use the work you completed in this unit to help you make your decisions.

- I can select and shape ideas to suit my purpose, adapting familiar forms and conventions.

- I can explore and connect ideas and choose the best way to plan my writing.

- I can produce thoughtful and imaginative texts to engage the reader.

SKILLS FOR LIFE

As a reward for coming top of the year, your teacher has organised a class trip to see the latest James Bond film. The cinema has sent the following email to your teacher reminding him of how children on school visits are expected to behave.

From: manager@cinesphere.co.uk

To: E.Scott@goosegoghigh.sch.gov
Subject: RE: School visit

We expect the highest standards of behaviour. Only refreshments purchased in the cinema are allowed and we definitely expect all rubbish to be picked up and taken away at the end of the screening. Mobile phones should be kept switched off at all times and no talking will be tolerated while the film is being shown. We have previously had an unfortunate incident with another school trip where pupils threw popcorn all around the cinema and we trust that this type of behaviour will not be exhibited by your pupils.

Your teacher has asked you to write an information sheet advising the class of the rules of behaviour that the cinema has set. Thinking about your audience, plan and draft the information sheet.

Writing AF2
Progress in ... Writing to suit your reader and purpose

LEARNING OBJECTIVES

- Draw on the conventions of different types of text to develop writing to fit specific tasks.
- Understand why writers use different levels of formality and use the appropriate style and register of English in your own writing.
- Understand the importance of standard English, and how to use it appropriately in your writing.

Activate your learning

Are there things that make you so angry you want to change them? Would you know how to write a letter that could make a difference?

Tom has seen a TV documentary about the way battery hens are treated so that the meat can be sold cheaply in supermarkets. He knows they will take his views seriously only if he uses the right level of formality in his letter.

1. a) Working in a group, make a list of the different ways you can create a formal tone in a letter. Think about:

    - the way you would start and end the letter

    - the vocabulary you would use

    - the types of sentences you would choose.

   b) Read Tom's thoughts. Decide what advice would you give him about how he should express these points in his letter.

> I think it's well minging the way farmers stuff thousands of battery hens into those dimly lit, cramped sheds. The bird only gets to live for 39 days and it's so sad – they get all that aggro – pecked at, squashed, having their beaks clipped and never get to live the way they're meant to. They should be larging it outside in the sunlight and eating proper food. A battery chicken only costs the supermarket 39p but they still charge the customer a couple of quid for it and we think 'That's cheap as chips' and buy it. It's bang out of order.

Language

c) Do you think Tom's language is formal or informal? Copy and complete the graph below, picking out any examples of standard or non-standard English.

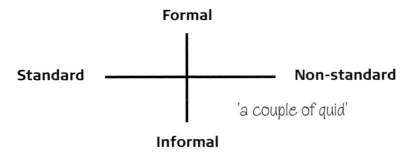

Formal

Standard ———————— **Non-standard**

'a couple of quid'

Informal

2 a) Using the advice you gave, write a letter to the supermarket. Think about the way you can express the points Tom made in a more formal way.

b) When you have drafted your letter, complete a table like the one below to compare the way Tom wrote down his thoughts with the way you expressed these in the letter.

The way Tom expressed the point in his thoughts	The way you expressed the same point in the letter
'well minging'	

Assess to Progress

How well can you write in standard English and use different levels of formality? Do you know when it is appropriate to use non-standard English such as dialect words or non-standard grammar? (Look at page 162 if you need to remind yourself of the difference between standard and non-standard English.)

Rate yourself for each of the skills below by deciding which number on the scale best shows your skill level.

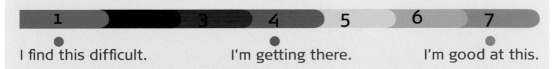

| 1 | 3 | 4 | 5 | 6 | 7 |

I find this difficult.   I'm getting there.   I'm good at this.

- I understand how important using standard English is and the ways it differs from non-standard English.

- I can make effective choices of how to write to suit different situations or to create particular effects.

Build your skills

Good writers know when to use standard and non-standard English to create appropriate levels of formality.

Use the skill steps to explore the language choices Benjamin Zephaniah has made in his poem 'Talking Turkeys'. Think about how you can apply these to your own writing.

Step 1 Decide on your purpose, audience and text type

When deciding on the appropriate level of formality for your writing and whether to use standard or non-standard English, you should consider:

- your **purpose** (why you are writing the text)
- your **audience** (the readers the text is aimed at)
- the **type of text** you are writing.

1   Read 'Talking Turkeys' opposite. Working with a partner, discuss:

- what Benjamin Zephaniah's purpose is – why do you think he has written this poem?
- who the audience for the text is – why do you think this?
- what type of text it is – how appropriate is the language he uses?

Support

To work out a text's **purpose**, ask yourself what the writer wants the reader to do, e.g. buy a product.

To work out the **audience**, try and find clues in the language a writer uses, e.g. a text that includes a lot of slang such as 'minging' and 'larging it' will probably be aimed at teenagers.

Talking Turkeys!

Be nice to yu turkeys dis christmas
Cos turkeys jus wanna hav fun
Turkeys are cool, an turkeys are wicked
An every turkey has a Mum.
Be nice to yu turkeys dis christmas,
Don't eat it, keep it alive,
It could be yu mate an not on yu plate
Say, Yo! Turkey I'm on your side.

I got lots of friends who are turkeys
An all of dem fear christmas time,
Dey say 'Benj man, eh, I wanna enjoy it,
But dose humans destroyed it
An humans are out of dere mind,
Yeah, I got lots of friends who are turkeys
Dey all hav a right to a life,
Not to be caged up an genetically made up
By any farmer an his wife.

Turkeys jus wanna play reggae
Turkeys jus wanna hip-hop
Havey you ever seen a nice young turkey saying,
'I cannot wait for de chop'?
Turkeys like getting presents, dey wanna watch
christmas TV,
Turkeys hav brains an turkeys feel pain
In many ways like yu an me.

I once knew a turkey His name was Turkey
He said 'Benji explain to me please,
Who put de turkey in christmas
An what happens to christmas trees?'
I said, 'I am not too sure Turkey
But it's nothing to do wid Christ Mass
Humans get greedy and waste more dan need be
An business men mek loadsa cash.'

So, be nice to yu turkey dis christmas
Invite dem indoors fe sum greens
Let dem eat cake an let dem partake
In a plate of organic grown beans,
Be nice to yu turkey dis christmas
An spare dem de cut of de knife,
Join Turkeys United an dey'll be delighted
An yu will mek new friends 'FOR LIFE'.

Step 2 Explore the effects of using standard or non-standard English

Standard English is the variety of English that is thought of by many as being 'correct' as it does not use slang or regional dialect words and is always **grammatically correct**. It makes the relationship between the writer and reader impersonal and distant.

Non-standard English uses **dialect words**, **slang** and different grammatical structures. Non-standard English is used in **informal** writing, when the writer and reader have a **personal** link.

1 a) Copy and complete the graph below. Where would you place the language Benjamin Zephaniah uses? Pick out examples and place them where you think they should go on the graph.

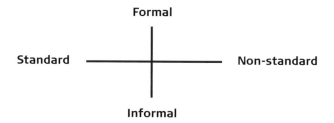

b) Highlight the phrase in the poem that you think is the most effective in persuading people not to eat turkeys. Discuss with a partner how the language used makes this effective.

2 a) Working with a partner use the information in the poem to write an introduction to a leaflet persuading families not to eat turkey at Christmas. Choose one stanza and rewrite it in standard English. You will need to change the slang or dialect words used, such as 'yu' for 'you' and 'mek' for 'make', and the structure of the sentences.

e.g. You should be nice to your turkeys this Christmas because turkeys just want to have fun ...

b) Compare your introduction with another pair's work and discuss the following questions:

● Do you think your version is as effective as the original in getting the message across?

● What do you think is lost by changing the style of English?

● Do you think anything has been gained by changing it?

Reinforce your skills

Choosing the right level of formality in your writing can be vital. A copywriter is paid by businesses to write texts that will appeal to readers. Choosing the wrong level of formality can lead to a lack of sales and demand for products.

Here are some briefs that a copywriter has received. You are going to use the skill steps you have practiced to help decide how formal each piece of writing needs to be.

A Client: Food magazine Brief:
A recipe for chicken aimed at busy people who don't usually cook and just want to be able to cook something easily when they get home from work.

B Client: Hospital Brief:
Information sheet explaining hip replacement operations to older patients.

C Client: Police Brief:
Advice leaflet for young people explaining what the law says about under-age drinking and the dangers involved.

A Client: Leisure Centre Brief:
Advertisement persuading teenagers to make more use of the leisure centre and including a special offer of two for the price of one entry and use of all facilities.

1   Work with a partner. As you read each brief, decide what you know about this type of text. Make a list of the typical features the copywriter could include.

2   Think about the purpose and audience for each text. What style of English do you think would be most appropriate? Be ready to give reasons for your choices.

3 For each brief, summarise your recommendations for the copywriter. Use a chart like the one below to make sure you include all the details the copywriter will need to help them write the texts.

Client	Leisure centre
Type of text	Advertisement
Audience	Teenagers
Purpose	Persuade them to come to the leisure centre
Standard or non-standard English	The advertisement could use some non-standard slang that would appeal to teenagers.
Level of formality	Use informal words and phrases to make it sound as though the leisure centre is friendly and aimed at them.

4 a) The copywriter has started to write the information sheet for the hospital. Read through the beginning of their first draft below and discuss whether you think the language choices made are correct.

Dodgy hip? Just chill out!

We can fit you with a new one in double-quick time. This will mean sharpening the old scalpel to whip out the old 'un before we bang in the new 'un, so you might be flat on your back for a good few weeks.

b) How would you adapt this to make it more appropriate for the target audience?

Extend your skills

Writers can make different choices about the level of formality they use even when they are writing for similar purposes and audiences.

1 a) Compare the following two recipes for chicken. Which do you think seems more informal?

b) Which recipe do you think would be most appropriate for Client A – the food magazine? Think about the effect the language used in each would have on the reader. Give reasons for your answer.

c) Rewrite the first recipe so that it uses the same style of language as the second recipe.

Baked chicken breasts

Ingredients

4 chicken breasts

1 tsp dried thyme

Olive oil

Method

1) Pre-heat the oven to 180°C/375°F/Gas mark 5

2) Place the chicken breasts into a baking dish, drizzle with the olive oil and sprinkle with the dried thyme. Cover and bake for 30–40 minutes until the chicken is thoroughly cooked – the meat must be white all the way through and the juices should run clear when a skewer is inserted into the thickest part of the chicken.

My basic roast chicken is the same as my mother's: I stick half a lemon up its bottom, smear some oil or butter on its breast, sprinkle it with a little salt, and put it in a Gas mark 6/200°C oven for about 20 minutes per 500g plus 30 minutes.

*From **How to Eat** by Nigella Lawson*

2 Swap the text you have written with a partner. Imagine you are somebody trying to make the recipe and make notes on:

- what effect the style of writing has on you as a reader – is it too informal?

- any words or phrases that you think don't keep to the same style (and suggest alternatives that would work better).

- whether it is easy to follow the recipe.

Stretch

Think about how you can mix and adapt the two different types of recipe you have explored and the features they use in order to meet your purpose. Think about the style of language you used. Did you include any examples of non-standard language to create specific effects?

Writing AF3
Progress in ... Experimenting with different ways of presenting texts

- Experiment with different ways of presenting texts on paper and on screen to suit the reader.
- Use different structures and approaches to ordering information and ideas to ensure that these are developed effectively across a text.
- Consider the reader's needs when choosing how to present and organise a text.

Activate your learning

1 Working in a group, match the following list of presentational features with the reason you think they are used:

Presentational features	Purpose
1 photographs	a to organise ideas
2 bullet points	b to make information easy to understand
3 bold and italic text	c to give emphasis
4 paragraphs	d to give visual interest
5 headings	e to signpost the reader
6 use of charts, graphs or tables	f to highlight key points

2 Read the advice text opposite. Work with a partner, to pick out and discuss each of the different presentational features used. How do they help the reader to understand the information? Are there any presentational features that you wouldn't expect to see in this type of article? Why do you think the writer used these?

3 Think about the following text types and discuss the kinds of presentational feature you expect to see in each.

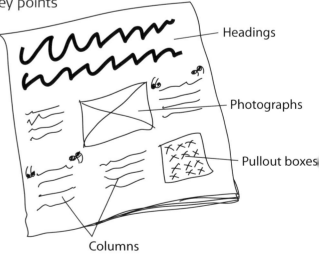

Headings

Photographs

Pullout boxes

Columns

a) a magazine article reviewing a new computer game.

b) instructions for a science experiment.

c) a letter saying you have won first prize in a free prize draw.

Saying Sorry

Should you apologise for a blunder?

$$D\left[R_p\left(R_a + P\right) + D\left(R_a - R_p\right)\right] = A$$

P = How annoyed is the person you may have upset?

D = How big a deal was your mistake? (1–10, where 10 = 'Our house is now a pile of rubble')

Ra = How responsible are you for this error of judgement? (1–10, where 10 = 'I left the gas on')

Rp = How responsible does your friend/boyfriend/girlfriend perceive you to be? (1–10, where 10 = 'Yes, you did leave the gas on')

What does it all mean?

- If A is less than 1, you do not need to apologise.
- If A is between 5 and 10, you should prepare a few remarks and deliver them with sincerity.
- If A is greater than 10, prepare to grovel.

Assess to Progress

Are you confident about how to present texts so that they will appeal to readers? Do you take care to organise your ideas and information in ways to suit different readers? Rate yourself for each of the skills below by deciding which number on the scale shows your skill level best.

| 1 | 2 | 3 | 4 | 5 | 6 | 7 |

I find this difficult.   I'm getting there.   I'm good at this.

- I can present texts on paper and on screen in different ways to suit different readers.

  Self-check: Do you have a blog or social networking page where you share information with friends? Do you add pictures and videos to entertain your readers?

- I can use different structures and ways of ordering information and ideas depending on the kind of text I am writing and who will read it.

  Self-check: When you are writing a report of an experiment in science, do you structure this in a different way from when you are writing a story in English?

- I understand and think carefully about my reader's needs when deciding how to present and organise my texts.

  Self-check: If you are writing the report of an event for your school newspaper, do you know how to use headlines and subheadings to guide the reader?

Reinforce your skills

The writer of the text opposite wants the readers of a magazine for teenage girls, *Mizz*, to support charities such as Guide Dogs for the Blind. Explore the ways the information is presented and organised by answering the questions below.

1 Consider the three main ideas the writer wants to present:

   - How the readers can support a charity.

   - Why donations for dog charities are needed.

   - How the money is used.

   Working with a partner, decide what order these ideas are presented in and how the order helps to achieve the writer's purpose.

The layout and presentational features used in a text can attract the reader's attention, emphasise information and guide the reader.

2 What presentational devices has the writer used on the page to:

   - separate out each idea?

   - make each idea stand out?

3 Read the *Togs for Dogs* mini-text. In what order does the writer give the information below?

   a) On *Togs for Dogs* day you can raise money in whatever way you like but mufti days are popular.

   b) This is how to contact the charity for an information pack.

   c) Raise money for the charity by supporting Togs for Dogs Day.

   d) There is a competition you can enter to raise money.

4 Using the information in the article, design a web page aimed at teenage readers. The web page should explain how to raise money for the charity. Think carefully about:

   - what information to include and what to leave out

   - the best way to organise the information for the reader

   - what presentational features to use so readers can find the most important information quickly

   - which presentational features will appeal to teenage readers.

WHY DONATE?

The government doesn't fund support dogs, so organisations rely on donations from people like you. Each dog costs from £10,000 or more to train and support for life, so cash is always desperately needed!

HERE'S HOW YOUR MONEY HELPS...

⭐ ___ a week can go towards training a puppy
⭐ ___ can help to rescue and train unwanted dogs
⭐ ___ buys a lead, collar and identity tag
⭐ ___ buys a jacket and harness for a guide dog
⭐ ___ pays to spay or neuter a dog, which helps it to stay calm and happy

Get involved with the Hearing Dogs For Deaf People's special **Togs For Dogs** campaign! Be a part of Togs For Dogs Day on Friday, 6th June 2008, and you can learn what it's all about, plus have loads of fun too.

There will be competitions, including one to design a jacket for cute Hearing Dog Jimmy. Time to get creative!

On the day itself, people can raise funds for Hearing Dogs in any way they choose. For schools taking part in previous years, the most popular scheme – unsurprisingly! – has been a 'mufti' or dress-down day, where you don't have to wear school uniform as long as you donate £1 to the charity.

It couldn't be easier to get your school, club or group, involved in Togs For Dogs 2008. Ask your teacher or group leader to get in touch with the charity to ask for an information pack. **Call 01844 348133, email togsfordogs@ hearingdogs.org.uk, or follow the links at www.hearingdogs.org.uk**

www.mizz.com **25**

Extend your skills

Being able to plan and develop a strong line of argument in a text is an important skill – especially if you want to persuade, complain or convince someone that your view is correct.

1   Read the text on page 174 and create a flow chart like the one below to show how the article's writer organised her ideas and used presentational devices to reinforce them.

a) For each paragraph draw a box and make a note of the idea or piece of information in it that the writer gives her readers.

b) Use arrows to show the order in which the writer gives these ideas and information.

c) Draw circles to add notes explaining how any connectives or linking phrases used shape the text and it's argument.

> Opening paragraph setting out a balanced view using phrases: 'While many claim ... some new research suggest ...'

Mobile phones: 2 Risky
Attention-grabbing heading. → Research – carrying mobile phones gives false sense of securuty →

Apply your learning

Working on your own, you are now going to use the skills you have developed through the unit to help you to complete the task below.

Task You have seen the following invitation on a website for teenagers:

Do you ever feel like yelling at someone but know you really shouldn't? Are your class-mates or family driving you mad? Do other people wind you up? Do you just want to have a whinge about your so called mate? Are all these questions making your blood boil? Well, this website is for people just like you ... instead of yelling at the wrong person, getting on your mum's nerves or boring your friends with all the things that make you mad, just log in here any time you want to have a moan, a whinge, let off steam or just have a rant at the end of a busy day ... sign-in and start your own web page (or post a comment on someone else's), you'll be so glad you did.

You have decided to write your own web page ranting about something that annoys you: this could be how people misuse mobile phones, people gossiping behind your back, anything that you feel strongly about.

Using the skills you have developed in this unit, plan, design and draft your web page. You need to:

● choose an appropriate style and tone that will appeal to your teenage audience and suit your purpose

● organise your text so that you build a strong line of argument to convince people of your point of view

● use different presentational features that will appeal to your readers and strengthen the points you are making

● create a layout that helps you to achieve your purpose and appeal to your readers.

Assess to Progress

Think about the tasks you have completed in this unit and especially the last one. How confident are you now about presenting and organising ideas and information in your own writing? Do you take care to organise your ideas and information in different ways to suit different readers? Look back at the ratings you gave on page 169. Now rate yourself again for each of the skills below by deciding which number on the scale best shows your skill level.

1   2   3   4   5   6   7

I find this difficult.   I'm getting there.   I'm good at this.

- I can present texts on paper and on screen in different ways to suit different readers.

- I can use different structures and ways of ordering information and ideas depending on the kind of text I am writing and who will read it.

- I understand and think carefully about my reader's needs when deciding how to present and organise my texts.

SKILLS FOR LIFE

Your school is running a series of events to celebrate Chinese New Year. The canteen staff are preparing a special lunch with five of your class's favourite Chinese dishes in it. As part of the fun, everyone will be given chopsticks to eat with.

Design and write an information poster to be put up outside the canteen. It must include the following information:

- why today's menu is all Chinese food
- what dishes are available on the menu and their prices
- a simple set of instructions explaining how to eat using chopsticks.

Progress in ... Using paragraphs and cohesive devices to develop and connect ideas

LEARNING OBJECTIVES

- Use paragraphs to develop and connect ideas in a way that supports the purpose of your writing.
- Use a range of techniques to create, develop and link ideas within paragraphs.
- Use a variety of links between paragraphs.

Activate your learning

Any good text should be easy to take apart sentence by sentence to see more clearly how it has been built. The following extract, from a wildlife magazine article about weasels, has been mixed up. Can you spot the links between sentences and work out the correct order?

A   This is because litters born in spring tend to stay with their families for the first two months after birth, so that they can learn all the necessary hunting skills.

B   Weasels can survive in a variety of habitats – woodlands, hedgerows, arable land, moorland and meadows – as long as there's plenty of prey and ground cover, so you may be lucky enough to spot one almost anywhere in mainland Britain.

C   For much of the year, weasels Mustela nivalis live solitary lives, but in summer you may see several of them together.

D   It sometimes goes after young rabbits, too, and is also partial to birds' eggs.

E   Despite rolling down the hedgebank and onto the path, the egg failed to break, so the weasel set about pushing it towards another precipice for a second attempt, with such single-minded determination – and probably with its vision obscured by the egg at the end of its nose – that it was quite oblivious to my presence.

F   In fact, some individuals have developed a remarkable technique for breaking open larger eggs, which I was once lucky enough to witness.

G   The weasel's super-slim build is a specialisation for hunting mice and voles as it has to follow its prey into their tiny nests and burrows.

H   A weasel suddenly appeared through a hedge, pushing a hen's egg along with its nose.

1   Working with a partner, read through the sentences and rearrange them into the right order. Copy them out in the right order, leaving space between each sentence to explain how it links to the previous sentence.

2   Now decide where the paragraph breaks should go.

Assess to Progress

How well can you use paragraphs already? Can you develop and connect ideas within and between your paragraphs? Rate yourself for each of the skills below, deciding where you feel you fit best on the scale. You should be able to give evidence for your decision, so think about the writing you have completed recently.

1	2	3	4	5	6	7

I find this difficult.   I'm getting there.   I'm good at this.

- I can use paragraphs to develop and connect ideas in a way that supports the purpose of my writing.

  Self-check: Can you use paragraphs to structure your writing, e.g. to give information, then to explain something, then to give a personal anecdote?

- I can use a range of techniques to create, develop and link ideas within paragraphs.

  Self-check: Do you know a range of different ways to link one sentence to the next, by using different connectives, or to build up ideas?

- I can link my paragraphs in a range of ways.

  Self-check: Do you know how to make the last sentence of a paragraph link to the first sentence of the next, e.g. by repeating the main topic word or another word or phrase with the same meaning?

Build your skills

When you write, it is important to use a range of ways to **link sentences and paragraphs** in order to develop and connect your ideas.

Read the following extract, taken from the opening of the novel *Exodus* by Julie Bertagna, and use the bullet points to help you explore the ways the ideas are linked within and between paragraphs.

Once upon a time there was a world...

... a world full of miracles. From the whirl of the tiniest particles to its spinning orbit in the unthinkable vastness of space, this world danced with miraculous life. Ur, the first people called their beautiful world, and the sound of that early name would carry down all the years, until aeons of time and tongues ripened Ur into Earth.

The people feasted upon their ripe world. Endlessly, they harvested its lands and seas. They grew greedy, ravaging the planet's bounty of miracles. Their waste and destruction spread like a plague until a day came when this plague struck at the very heart of the miraculous dance. And the people saw, too late, their savage desolation of the world.

The globe grew hot and fevered, battered by hurricanes and rain. Oceans and rivers rose to drown the cities and wasted lands. Earth raged with a century of storm. Then came a terrible calm. Imagine survivors scattered upon lonely peaks, clinging to the tips of skyscrapers, to bridges and treetops.

Now retrack to the dawn of the world's drowning. Stand at the fragile moment before the devastation begins, and wonder. Is this where we stand now, right here on the brink?

- In the first paragraph, the writer uses the noun 'miracles' and repeats the adjective 'miraculous' from the same word family to develop the idea of the world being amazing.

- The first paragraph introduces the 'first people' and the second paragraph develops the description of them using pronouns and repetition 'The people feasted', 'they harvested' and 'They grew greedy'.

- The use of synonyms (words that mean the same thing) to refer to the Earth like 'world', 'planet' and 'globe' coupled with words such as 'bounty' and 'ripe', extends and adds to the idea of plenty.

- Antonyms (words with opposite meanings) are used in the second paragraph to contrast with the plentiful images and introduce the theme of 'waste' and 'destruction'.

1 How do the different ways the writer links her ideas within each paragraph as well as across them help you to understand the events being described? Discuss the way she uses:

- the noun, adjective and verb form of a word, such as 'dance' and 'danced' or 'miracles' and 'miraculous'

- synonyms, or other word types of the synonym, such as 'harvest' and 'bounty'

- antonyms of some words, such as 'waste' and 'destruction'

- similar noun phrases, such as 'a world', 'this world', 'their beautiful world'

- temporal (time) connectives such as 'once upon a time' and 'until'.

2 How does she use time as a way of linking each paragraph? How does this help the reader to understand the changes she describes?

3 a) Working in pairs, link the ideas in the following sentences, taken from a textbook describing how the Earth was formed. The sentences are in chronological order. You should use the techniques you have explored to help you to:

- replace the simple nouns with synonyms, pronouns or noun phrases

- add temporal connectives or references to time

- organise the sentences into paragraphs to help the reader understand the process.

> The Earth was a ball of hydrogen and helium which condensed.
> The Earth was a liquid ball of molten rock.
> Small space rocks collided with it and formed the planet.
> The Earth began to cool.
> A thin crust formed on its surface.
> Water vapour evaporated and condensed to form the atmosphere.
> Clouds formed and there were many storms.
> The rain cooled the planet.
> Oceans and rivers formed.

b) Compare your text with another pair's version. How helpful does the other pair find the way you have linked and connected the ideas?

Reinforce your skills

Some writers, for example, journalists, have to be able to **develop ideas** in short pieces of writing and use different techniques to help **build their argument**. The article below explains why the Liverpool should be the European Capital of Culture. Read the text and answer questions below to help you explore the text.

1   How does the opening paragraph introduce the idea of comparing Liverpool and Manchester?

Liverpool, universally remembered for *Brookside*, the shell suit wearing 'scousers' from *The Harry Enfield Show* and 'dey do, doh, don't dey doh?', has never had the luck of its neighbour, Manchester. While Manchester is seen as 'cool', Liverpool hasn't been able to shake off the stereotypes and celebrate the global impact of local talent. To many, Liverpool is little more than red or blue-shirted football fans and 'scallies'.

2   Read the next two paragraphs.

a)   Sum up in one sentence what they are about.

b)   Why do you think the writer has put the paragraphs in this order? How do they link together?

Manchester always seems to have picked up the cool crowd, like 'Madchester' in the 1980s, with bands like The Happy Mondays, New Order and The Stone Roses. It's a city that's always been associated with cool music. Even Oasis did little to ruin the myth of the cool, swaggering Manc.

So why can't Liverpool rise above the stereotypes to claim the Capital of Cool? It has its own deeply cool music scene, including being the home of The Zutons and The Coral. Not that it needs to depend on its current music scene, either.

3 a) Read the next two paragraphs below. How does the writer build up links between these paragraphs?

b) How does putting the paragraphs in this order help the writer's purpose in writing the column? Discuss your ideas with a partner.

4 a) What does the writer want the readers to think after reading the last paragraph?

b) How do the ideas link together in this paragraph? Pick out where examples have been used to develop an idea.

And it's not just the music. Liverpool's docklands are a UNESCO World Heritage Site, recognising their importance as a commercial capital in the eighteenth century. Sure, Manchester was important, too, but it's not a World Heritage Site. Liverpool has historical status behind its modern-day culture.

And there's one area where the country looks to when thinking about sport: the North West. Football might not mean culture to you, but to millions of people, it's as much a part of life as music, art or history. Manchester United have dominated football for some years, but Liverpool's own teams have always put up a more than resilient fight and one of Liverpool's boys is now universally accepted as one of the best players in the sport's history – Wayne Rooney.

So why should Liverpool be the Capital of Culture? It's as much about being proud of its achievements as it is about culture. Here's a city that has come through bombings in World War II, mass unemployment as the docks closed and national ridicule. The worst has happened to Liverpool and it has come back stronger than ever. It's as much a reward for the resilience of Liverpudlians as it is a reward for culture.

5 Working in pairs, you are going to develop the ideas in the text by adding your own paragraphs about the following points:

- Liverpool has Aintree racecourse where the Grand National horse race is run.

- Liverpool is the only city to have had a football club in the top league every single year since the leagues formed in 1888.

- *Hollyoaks*, one of the best soap operas on television, is filmed in Liverpool. It was the only soap nominated in every category in the 2007 British Soap Awards.

Develop one idea by adding an example that supports what you say and another by presenting the opposing idea or comparing it with what happens in another town.

Extend your skills

Another way writers can develop ideas in their paragraphs is by using a **cause and effect pattern**.

1 Read the following passage in which David Attenborough explains the process of how snow carves the earth's landscape. Answer the questions around the text to help you explore the techniques he uses to build up his paragraph.

a) Is the opening sentence a cause or an effect?

b) How does the writer organise sentences 2-4?

c) Why does the writer use these temporal connectives in this order?

The snow flakes, falling so gently on the mountains of the world, are agents of destruction. They mantle the peaks in fields metres deep. Their lower layers, compressed by the weight above, turn to ice. It closes around projections of rock and penetrates the cracks and joints. As the snow continues to fall above, the ice beneath begins to move slowly down the steep slopes under its own weight, dragging away plates and blocks of rock as it goes. Most of the time, the movement is so slow that its only visible signs are widening cracks across the snowfield. On occasion, the whole sheet suddenly loses its grip and thousands of tons of ice, snow and rocks sweep down the mountain.

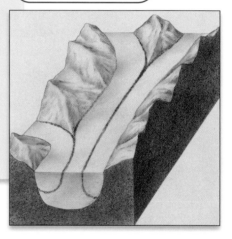

2 Draw and label this diagram to show the process the writer explains in this paragraph.

3 a) Now read the next paragraph below. What linking techniques does David Attenborough use in order to develop his ideas?

   b) What links does he make between sentences in order to develop the explanation of the effect of the water? How might you be able to use these in your writing?

All this frozen water, gathering in the vast couloirs between the mountain ridges, unites to form a river of ice, a glacier. Now the destruction becomes devastating. As the glacier slides downwards, it scrapes away at the sides of the valley against which it presses. Beneath, boulders frozen into its underside, like teeth in a gigantic rasp, grind down its bed. Ahead, it pushes a huge wall of shattered rock. Slowly it inches downwards below the level of permanent snow until the warmth begins to melt it, and water, creamy with pulverised stone, gushes from its snout.

GLOSSARY

couloirs – corridors
rasp – metal file
pulverised – mashed up

3 Now look at the following ideas taken from the next paragraph. Write a paragraph linking these together, thinking about how each sentence explains the effect of carving out our landscape. Remember, you will also need to use a range of ways to link the sentences across the paragraphs.

> Rain also contributes to the destruction of the landscape.
>
> Rain falls and works its way into rock crevices.
>
> The rain freezes in these crevices at night.
>
> The ice expands and breaks off fragments of loose rock.
>
> In the day, the rain melts again and runs down into rivers, carrying the rock sediment with it.

Support

These sentences use the word 'rain' four times. Think about ways you could structure your paragraph to avoid repetition.

Try to use different temporal connectives to join some of the sentences together. Think about where you could add the following time phrases:
- 'As the sun rises again and warms the earth ...'
- 'Throughout the year ...'

Stretch

Look at the order of the sentences. Here, David Attenborough outlines an effect, the destruction of the landscape, and then explains the causes that lead to this. If your purpose was to build up to the effect, how might you rearrange the order of this information rather than give it away immediately? Rewrite your paragraph so that it builds up to the final effect.

4 Swap your writing with a partner's and explain the techniques you have used to link sentences together and build up your explanation.

When developing your own writing, you can use different planning formats to help you to arrange the paragraphs in a logical order, for example using a fishbone diagram.

5 Look back over the text you have read in this section and the paragraph you added to it. 'Reverse plan' the text to show what a plan might look like for these paragraphs.

Apply your learning

Working on your own, you are now going to use the skills you have developed through the unit to help you to complete the task below.

In 1949, George Orwell wrote a novel called *Nineteen Eighty-Four*, which introduced the idea of 'Room 101'. Room 101 is a room for torture, where all the things you hate or are afraid of are kept to torture you. It's the inspiration behind the television series *Room 101* where celebrities nominate things they would like to get rid of for ever.

Task You have been asked to write a column in your school magazine in which you describe and explain what you would like to put in Room 101.

1 Before you begin to write, decide on four or five ideas you could write about and make a note of these. Remember, your purpose is to describe and explain, so you will need to make it clear why you think a particular thing should be banished for ever. The school magazine is read by pupils, parents and teachers, so make sure your ideas are not too controversial.

2 Once you have chosen one idea to write about, plan your writing using a format that will help you to decide how to link and develop your ideas. You might want to start with your most convincing idea and develop it from there, or you may wish to build up to your most convincing idea so you can end your column powerfully.

3 As you write your column, think carefully about how you use paragraphs to develop and connect your ideas in a way that suits the purpose of your writing. Try to use different techniques to create links within and between paragraphs. Think about:

- how you are going to extend your paragraphs and show you can add explanations, explain effects and use examples

- how to use a range of linking devices such as synonyms, antonyms, temporal connectives and contrasting ideas to link your paragraphs

- making sure your paragraphs are organised effectively to help the reader follow your line of argument.

Assess to Progress

How well can you now use and link paragraphs? Look back at the ratings you gave on page 179. Now rate yourself again for each of the skills below. Pick out examples that show your skill level from the writing you have completed in this unit.

- I use paragraphs to develop and connect ideas in a way that supports the purpose of my writing.

- I use a range of techniques to create, develop and link ideas within paragraphs.

- I use a variety of links between paragraphs.

Now answer the following questions.

1   What have you learned that you did not know or could not do before?

2   What was the hardest part of this unit?

SKILLS FOR LIFE

Your local shopping centre has decided to ban children or adults who are wearing hooded tops, saying that they are often anti-social. They have taken statements from four shop owners and need to put these into a press release explaining why they have implemented the ban.

1   Write the press release explaining the reasons behind the ban.

▪ Decide on an order for these different statements and how you would organise them into paragraphs.

▪ Think of the ways you could link sentences within and between paragraphs.

When CCTV captures people shoplifting, they can't be identified easily, so it's hard to prosecute them.	When you can't see people's faces, it can be very threatening and intimidating.
This is a protective measure so we can protect our staff and customers.	It's not so much the hood that's the problem, but the way people use it to conceal their faces.

Writing AF5

Progress in ... Applying knowledge of sentence lengths and structures

LEARNING OBJECTIVES

- Use a variety of sentence lengths and structures, including complex sentences, to help the reader understand your ideas.
- Use a variety of sentences to create effects that are appropriate for the purpose of your writing.
- Carefully manage the tense you are writing in.
- Use modal verbs to control the tone of your writing.

Activate your learning

1 Read the following sentences then look at the author's explanations about how each sentence was constructed. Match each explanation to the sentence you think the author has written.

a) It will be cloudy with some outbreaks of sunshine and rain.

b) Rainy day, much worse than expected, cricket match cancelled.

c) The thunder and lightning, driven from the North East and the North West, battered down on rooftop and treetop all day and into the night.

d) As she crept out of the prison others called school, the clouds gathered together and threatened to spread rumours of her flight.

e) Far out. This was beyond the realm they had previously experienced; it was the Kromer zone.

f) The sky, which suggested the dawn of another troubled day, glowered at him.

1. I like using pace so the reader gets information in stages.

2. I like making my reader think of two things at the same time. It keeps them alert.

3. I like creating drama by going over the top with extra bits of information at all points in my sentences.

4. I like to control how my text is read. I like using punctuation carefully – it's like my breathing apparatus.

5. I was making notes in my diary. I write down the basics.

6. I need to get the information across quickly in a way that's easy to understand.

2 a) Use the picture above to inspire some creative sentences of your own. Try creating:

- a sentence of mystery by starting with 'It was ...'

- a sentence of power by declaring 'It will ...'

- a sentence of uncertainty by guessing 'It might ...'

b) Explain to your partner how you created your sentences and what effect you wanted them to have.

Assess to Progress

How well can you make sure that your sentences say what you want them to say? Do you vary the sentences you use to create different effects for your readers? Look at the skills listed in the table and, for each row, decide which statement fits you best.

When I create a sentence ...

I make some attempt to vary length, structure and subject.	I use a variety of lengths, structures and subjects to make my meanings clear.	I control the lengths, structures and subjects of my sentences to help me to achieve my purpose as a writer.
I try to use connectives such as 'and' or 'but' to make my sentences longer.	I use a wider range of connectives to link my ideas together.	I try to craft the way details are given to the reader by using connectives in interesting ways.
I try to check that the verbs I use suit my purpose and that the tense is correct.	I make sure that I use the most effective verbs and stick to the right tense.	I use verbs in a particular way to create extra meaning in my writing.

Build your skills

Effective writers choose the right types of sentence by matching the length, structure and subject to the type of text they are writing.

1 Working with a partner, discuss what types of sentences you would expect to use in the following writing situations:

- Writing a new paragraph for an adventure story
- Writing a letter of complaint
- Writing a persuasive speech for a politician
- Writing a prescription for a patient
- Writing a crime report
- Writing instructions about how to respond to a fire alarm

Work through the skill steps to explore how to make effective choices when writing for different purposes.

Step 1 Use short, simple sentences

When you want to give information quickly, speed up the pace, or make a reader stop and think, using short, simple sentences can be helpful.

1 a) Working with a partner, read the following examples and decide which type of text from the list above each writer is writing:

> Leave by the nearest fire exit.
> Do not run.
> Do not collect your belongings.
> Make your way to the assembly point.

> The weather was the vilest George had experienced since moving to the island six years ago. No one was out of doors. Rain battered against the windows, making sleep impossible and threatening to … Crash!

b) Discuss the effect that using short, simple sentences has in each of the texts.

> e.g. In the first text, the writer is trying to be clear and simple so has used short, simple sentences …

2 Which other writing situations do you think using short, simple sentences would be appropriate for? Choose one other text type from the list and work with your partner to draft the opening paragraph.

Step 2 Use complex sentences

When you want to give information in a way that engages your reader, using complex sentences can be helpful. These can be effective when used

in non-fiction texts to help the reader understand exactly what the writer means and in fiction to make the reader aware of something unusual or a change.

1   Discuss the following two examples with your partner. What kind of text do you think each writer is writing? What effect do the complex sentences have on you as a reader?

A The barometer, <u>which</u> is an instrument that detects the smallest change in atmosphere, suggests that we are indeed heading for a storm of the greatest magnitude. We need to act fast.

B The sky, <u>which</u> felt like it was sinking down on top of them, turned grey and the waves, <u>which</u> were leaping up at them like hyenas, started to seep onto the deck.

Support

Notice how both writers uses a comma and the word 'which' to trigger extra information in the middle of their sentences.

2   Choose another writing situation from the list on page 190 where you think using complex sentences would be helpful. Working with a partner, draft an opening paragraph that uses complex sentences to give more information to the reader.

Support

A complex sentence has two or more clauses that are joined by a connective or a punctuation mark.

Ellie and Daniel are studying **because** *they have a test tomorrow.*

Think about the range of punctuation marks and the different connectives you can use to trigger more information in your opening paragraph: e.g. 'which', 'where', 'who', 'although'.

Step 3   Construct sentences to create different effects

The way you construct your sentences can make a big difference to the meaning created and the effect they have on your reader. Look at the following sentences, taken from a letter of complaint.

Due to the disgraceful state of the pavement along Baldwin Road, my neighbour has suffered countless trips and stumbles outside his home.

Despite the numerous letters, telephone calls and visits to your offices, my neighbour has received no information about when the pavement will be repaired.

Although he is struggling to make ends meet and in far from good health, my neighbour has had to sort this problem out himself.

Putting the main clause at the end of each sentence and packing information at the front gives these sentences real impact. Choosing the right connective also helps to connect the ideas and make the writer's meaning clear.

1 a) Read the sentences aloud in pairs. Now swap the clauses around so each one begins with 'My neighbour' and read them aloud again.

   b) What effect did swapping the clauses have? Which order do you think is best used if the writer wants just to give information? Which order creates a persuasive effect? Give reasons for your answers.

2 Think of other times when using this technique might be helpful, such as in an advertising campaign. Working with a partner, create same sentences that will have a powerful impact on the reader. Try using connectives to link your sentences:

● two ideas linked by being similar: 'Moreover'.

● two ideas linked by being dependent on the other: 'Hence', Therefore, 'Thus'.

● two ideas linked by being different: 'Nevertheless'.

Reinforce your skills

Look at the extract opposite from a short science fiction story about time travel called *A Sound of Thunder* by Ray Bradbury. The characters have travelled far back in time. As you read, think about the sentences the writer uses to create suspense and excitement.

1 How does the writer vary his sentences to create a sense of the setting? Create a list of examples of short, simple sentences and long, complex sentences that help to build up a sense of place.

   e.g. 'The Machine Stopped.' – the short, simple sentence creates a dramatic pause.

The Machine slowed; its scream fell to a murmur. The Machine stopped.

The sun stopped in the sky.

The fog that had enveloped the Machine blew away and they were in an old time, a very old time indeed, three hunters and two Safari Heads with their blue metal guns across their knees.

'Christ isn't born yet,' said Travis, 'Moses has not gone to the mountains to talk with God. The Pyramids are still in the earth, waiting to be cut out and put up. Remember that. Alexander, Caesar, Napoleon, Hitler – none of them exists.' The man nodded. 'That' – Mr. Travis pointed – 'is the jungle of sixty million two thousand and fifty-five years before President Keith.'

He indicated a metal path that struck off into green wilderness, over streaming swamp, among giant ferns and palms.

'And that,' he said, 'is the Path, laid by Time Safari for your use. It floats six inches above the earth. Doesn't touch so much as one grass blade, flower, or tree. It's an anti-gravity metal. Its purpose is to keep you from touching this world of the past in any way. Stay on the Path. Don't go off it. I repeat. Don't go off. For any reason! If you fall off, there's a penalty. And don't shoot any animal we don't okay.'

'Why?' asked Eckels.

They sat in the ancient wilderness. Far birds' cries blew on a wind, and the smell of tar and an old salt sea, moist grasses, and flowers the color of blood.

'We don't want to change the Future. We don't belong here in the Past. The government doesn't like us here. We have to pay big graft to keep our franchise. A Time Machine is finicky business. Not knowing it, we might kill an important animal, a small bird, a roach, a flower even, thus destroying an important link in a growing species.'

2   Draft your own sentences that would help to create a sense of the setting in the story on page 193. Then replace some of the author's original sentences with your own.

3   Now choose one of the titles below and write the opening paragraph of your own science fiction story. You should use sentences that help you to create a sense of your story's setting. Think about the different sentence types and lengths Ray Bradbury uses in his story.

The Blur Of Mist   **Depths of Darkness**

The Haze of Sunshine

A Flash of Lightning

4   Working in a group of four, read each other's paragraphs. Discuss the sentences used and the different effects these create. Does reading the other story openings give you any ideas about improvements you could make to your own?

Stretch

Think about how you can use punctuation marks such as the semi-colon or the dash to trigger more information in the sentences you create, e.g.

The Machine slowed; its scream fell to a murmur.

Language

Extend your skills

As well as using different sentence types, good writers need to be able to manage the tense they write in effectively and use the correct forms of verbs in their writing. Read the following article about sneezing and then look at the annotations to explore the way the writer has done this.

Sneezing into sleeve stops germs spreading

> Reporting that something has been said is in the past tense to show that the words were said at some point earlier.

'Traditional advice to cover the mouth and nose actually encourages the spread of disease', said Prof John Oxford, 'because viruses are easily spread through touch'.

He claimed that by sneezing and coughing into the crook of the elbow or the sleeve, those with colds can minimise the spread of germs.

Prof Oxford, of Queen Mary Medical School in London, also said that basic hygiene measures have been forgotten in the fight against everyday infections, with sufferers increasingly looking to science to cure their ills.

Ditching handkerchiefs in favour of disposable tissues also helps, but regularly washing hands with soap and water is most important, he told the *Daily Telegraph*.

Prof Oxford said: 'The new etiquette should be to cough and sneeze into your elbow. It breaks the chain of transmission and you must wash your hands properly and regularly. You should sing *Happy Birthday* twice over while washing your hands with hot water and soap, a quick squirt of cold water will not do it. The handkerchief can be a harbinger of unpleasant micro-organisms. Bacteria can multiply in them.'

> Reporting what someone said in the present tense to show that the opinions is still held.

> The professor uses modal verbs to emphasise how important his instructions are.

1 Working with a partner, find other examples of verbs in the past and present tenses and decide why they have been used.

2 Working in a group, role-play a discussion between the professor, the reporter and a reader. Use the following questions to discuss in role the issue of sneezing. One member of the group should listen to the role play and make notes about the way tenses are used.

Language

Modal verbs such as 'will', 'can', 'shall', 'may', 'should', 'could', 'would', 'might' and 'must' are auxiliary verbs that can be used to express:

● the future, e.g. 'we will go … '

● possibilities, e.g. 'we could go …'

● demands, e.g. 'we must go …'.

3 Look again at the article on page 195. Working with a partner, make a list of the modal verbs that the professor uses. Try reading the sentences without the modal verb and discuss how this changes the tone.

4 Try using the modal verbs to change the tone of the following two sentences.

● Viruses are easily spread through touch.

● Ditching handkerchiefs in favour of disposable tissues also helps.

a) Which modal verb could you add to make the statements more forceful?

| will | can | shall | should |

b) Which modal verb could you add to make the statements more hesitant?

| could | would | might | must |

5 Look back at the list of writing situations on page 190. In which text would it be appropriate to use modal verbs? Write the opening of this text, using modal verbs to make the meaning clear to the reader.

Apply your learning

Task You are going to write two different texts. Remember to think about the type of text you are writing and vary the sentences you use, selecting different lengths and types of sentences to suit your purpose and audience.

1 You have been asked to create the introduction to a health leaflet warning elderly people about the dangers of flu, which leads to the deaths of 25,000 people each year. This introduction needs to explain how to avoid spreading germs. You should aim to write at least six sentences and think carefully about how you could emphasise the importance of your advice.

2 You have been asked to write the opening scene for a science fiction story. Aliens have landed and the inhabitants of Earth suspect that they are about to suffer the outbreak of a killer virus. Aim to write about half a page including dialogue and think carefully about how you could make the setting and characters seem strange.

Assess to Progress

How good are you now at varying the sentences you use to suit the purpose and audience for your writing? Look back at the skills statements on page 189. Choose one box from each row of the table that best describes your skill level now. Discuss your choices with a partner and explain how you have proved this in the writing you have just completed.

SKILLS FOR LIFE

You have won a competition at your school to trial a new mobile phone. The phone, which is priced at £129.99, has a built-in camera and gives high-speed broadband Internet access.

Overall, you were quite impressed with the phone, although some of the features didn't work that well: the address book didn't scroll quickly enough and the number pad had a habit of sticking.

In order to keep the phone, you need to write a clear and informative report for the phone company on your two weeks' trial. You need to explain the good and bad features of the phone and the reasons why you think it is worth having.

Progress in ... Using a range of punctuation for clarity and effect

LEARNING OBJECTIVES

- Use correct punctuation within and between sentences, using colons and semi-colons to clarify meaning and create a variety of effects.
- Write speech using correct punctuation.
- Craft language, using syntax and punctuation accurately within sentences for expression and effect in different types of writing.
- Develop your editing and proofreading skills to improve your writing as you review and revise.

Activate your learning

Here is the first draft of a survey to find out which female R&B artist is the most popular.

1   To show how much you already know about punctuation, rewrite the text using all the punctuation marks from the chart below. Make sure you also add capital letters where they are needed.

As part of our poll choose your favourite R&B performer from the following j lo jennifer lynn lopez sold over 50 million records worldwide won american music awards favourite latin artist it was rumoured that j lo became a scientologist but just prior to those reports she said to nbc I'm not a scientologist i was raised catholic fergie stacey ann ferguson lead vocalist for the black eyed peas won american music awards favourite female artist rihanna robyn rihanna fenty grammy award winning singer from barbados one of the four richest young people in hollywood beyonce beyonce giselle knowles lead vocalist in destinys child the worlds best selling female group of all time debut album sold 317000 copies in the first week mariah carey mariah carey has had 17 no 1 singles has at least a five octave vocal range what an amazing group to choose from do you need to know more

.	,	:	;	!	?	(	)	"	'	-

2   Working with a partner, create your own survey to find which male artists are the most popular in your class. Think about ways you can use punctuation to help make your survey easy to understand and complete.

Assess to Progress

How good are you at using a range of punctuation in your own writing? Can you use punctuation to help make meaning clear for your reader or to create particular effects? Thinking about the task you have just completed, decide how you would rate yourself for the following skills using the scale below.

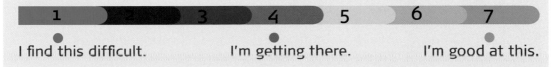

1   2   3   4   5   6   7

I find this difficult.   I'm getting there.   I'm good at this.

- I can use full stops, capital letters, commas, apostrophes, question marks and exclamation marks accurately.

- I know when I should use semi-colons and colons and can use these correctly when writing different types of sentence.

- I am confident when punctuating speech.

- I proofread my work at different stages and use my editing skills to improve my writing when I review and revise it.

Build your skills

Punctuation shapes and alters meaning and helps other people to understand what we have written: sentences need to be carefully constructed and they need signposts to let the reader know how to navigate them.

Using a wide range of punctuation can help a writer to present information to a reader in different ways. For example, you can:

Use a semi-colon (;) to:

- join different clauses (parts of a sentence that make sense independently) together to show they are closely linked, e.g. 'I am very keen on playing snooker; Tom prefers playing pool'.

- separate items in a list, e.g. 'When I went shopping I bought: a T-shirt; a pair of trainers; the new CD by Rihanna and a magazine'.

Use a colon (:) to:

- show that some information is to follow; it could be a list, a statement or a saying.

Language

Read the article below which gives advice and information about sleeping well.

1   Working with a partner, answer the questions around the text.

2   Join with another pair and compare your answers. Were there any answers that you disagreed about?

Sleep

a) Explain the different ways that commas are used in this passage.

A spokesman for sleep research has recently stated, 'Up to two thirds of school children don't get as much sleep as they should, and this can make them stressed and slow at school. Young people are supposed to get a good 8 to 10 hours each night, but many children have missed out on 4,500 vital hours of shut-eye by the time they are age seven.'

b) What punctuation marks are used to show someone is starting to speak?

c) If there had been more than one researcher, would you change this punctuation?

The researcher's advice is as follows:

d) Why is a colon used here?

*   try to go to bed and get up at the same time everyday;

*   don't sleep late the next day because you've had a bad night;

e) Why is the semi-colon used here?

*   avoid caffeine eg in chocolate, tea, soft drinks, coffee;

*   give yourself time to write down concerns.

And finally, don't eat too much before bedtime; take regular exercise during the day.

g) How is the semi-colon used differently here?

Have you ever tried to get to sleep by counting sheep? It doesn't work, does it That's because counting sheep is too boring, say two Oxford scientists. The two researchers took 50 people who have trouble getting to sleep:

f) What punctuation mark is missing here?

*   one third were asked to count sheep;

*   one third tried to imagine a beach or a waterfall;

*   the rest were asked not to do either, so they could compare the results.

Apart from the few who needed the toilet, those imagining the waterfall fell asleep 20 minutes earlier than usual. The sheep counters actually stayed awake longer than usual!

h) Why does the writer use a punctuation mark here?

When you are writing, the first thing you need to think about is who you are writing for and why you are writing, as this will influence the sort of sentences you choose to write and how you punctuate them. Using the skill steps below will help you to do this.

Step 1 Use a variety of sentence shapes to create effect

Knowing how and when to use different types of punctuation gives you confidence that you can create and control different types and lengths of sentence.

1 Working with a partner, discuss the ways that the punctuation used in the article opposite helps to make the advice clear to the reader. Pick out one example that shows this.

Step 2 Use punctuation to link ideas and build detail

Reread the opening sentence of the article on page 200. Notice how the writer uses punctuation to link the ideas that many children don't get enough sleep and that this can make them stressed and slow at school.

1 Use a combination of punctuation marks and connectives to link the following sentences:

- Children need 8 to 10 hours' sleep a night.
- They can get stressed if they have too little sleep.
- They need sleep to be attentive at school.
- TV is often blamed.

Step 3 Use more advanced punctuation, such as colons and semi-colons

1 Punctuate these sentences using the colon and semi-colon, rewording them as necessary.

a) The following is good advice don't eat too much before bedtime take regular exercise during the day.

b) To get a good night's sleep you need to remember not to drink caffeine before you go to bed to keep regular hours get anything that might be worrying you off your mind.

c) Harry realised lack of sleep could be serious as a stressful attitude and slowness at school might occur.

2 Working with a partner, compare how you have used punctuation in each sentence. Explain the choices you made and the reasons for these.

Reinforce your skills

Now practise the skill steps to write a review using a wide range of punctuation to present information clearly to your reader.

The text below is a fact file giving information about the Doctor Who Christmas special, *The Voyage of the Damned*. Using the details given, write a 300-word review of the programme for *Top DVD* magazine encouraging readers to buy it.

Fact File: Dr Who – The Voyage of the Damned

Series:	**Christmas Special 2007**
Doctor:	Tenth Doctor – David Tennant
Companion:	Astrid Path – Kylie Minogue
Enemy:	Host of Heaven; Max Capricorn
Setting:	London 2008, aboard the *Titanic*
Writer:	Russell T Davies
Ratings:	13.31 million

Plot:
- Spaceship Titanic visits Earth at Christmas
- Ship damaged by sabotage of captain and meteors
- Extinction level collision with Earth imminent
- Android 'Host' sets out to kill all survivors on board
- Doctor saved by Astrid – she dies in the attempt
- Doctor averts collision – saves the world

Character of the Doctor:
- Boundless enthusiasm and energy
- Behaviour often manic and inappropriate
- Often driven by anger or belief he is right
- Feels for those who suffer – often lonely
- Enthralled by wonders of technology
- Thinks life is brilliant

What viewers thought of the Voyage of the Damned
Dan: A really great adventure.
Katy: I thought it was brilliant. It was scary, creepy, funny, sad and action all at the same time.
Jack: I thought it was all right but not as good as the one with Catherine Tate.
Nosheen: Links with the original *Titanic* were good.

1 Working with a partner, plan your review. Think about what you will need to include and how you can organise the information given.

2 Draft your review of the programme. As you write, think about how you should use punctuation to present the details.

- Plot – think about how you can use punctuation to link these details into an effective summary.

- Describe the characters – you could list the Doctor's characteristics.

- Viewer's comments – remember to punctuate speech correctly.

Use the final skill step below help you to check that your review makes sense and is as accurate as possible.

Step 4 Proofread to check that your work makes sense and that spelling and punctuation are accurate

When reviewing your writing, try to get some distance from what you have written to look at it with a fresh eye – as a reader rather than as a writer. Sometimes asking a partner to read your writing can also help.

Read your work out loud or 'out loud in your head', or try reading it backwards. If you spot any sentences that are awkward or confusing, highlight these. When you have finished proofreading, find a different way of expressing your idea and edit your text to make this improvement.

It is important when reviewing your work to know what your weaknesses are and to check for one thing at a time:

- For meaning – Does what you have written makes sense?

- For spelling – Have you spotted any spelling errors?

- For punctuation – does your punctuation help to make your review clear and link your ideas effectively?

1 Review and revise your writing. Pay particular attention to the punctuation you have used and make sure that you try to include a wide range of effective punctuation.

Extend your skills

So far you have looked at how punctuation can be used in non-fiction texts to help link ideas together and make these clear for the reader. Writers of fiction also use punctuation to create specific effects that can grab a reader's attention and keep them reading.

The text below is the opening to the novel *Bleak House* by the Victorian author, Charles Dickens, where London is covered in a blanket of fog. Read the text, and see if you can spot any of the punctuation techniques you have explored so far in the unit. There might be words you are not familiar with, but try to focus on how Dickens has shaped and punctuated his sentences.

> The simple, blunt opening gives a snapshot view of London.

> We have two long sentences here broken up with semi-colons. They add much greater detail in the form of a list – fog entering everything from ships' cabins to the eyes and throats of old people.

Fog everywhere. Fog up the river, where it flows among green aits and meadows; fog down the river, where it rolls deified among the tiers of shipping and the waterside pollutions of a great (and dirty) city. Fog on the Essex marshes, fog on the Kentish heights. Fog creeping into the cabooses of collier-brigs; fog lying out on the yards and hovering in the rigging of great ships; fog drooping on the gunwales of barges and small boats. Fog in the eyes and throats of ancient Greenwich pensioners, wheezing by the firesides of their wards; fog in the stem and bowl of the afternoon pipe of the wrathful skipper, down in his close cabin; fog cruelly pinching the toes and fingers of his shivering little 'prentice boy on deck. Chance people on the bridges peeping over the parapets into a nether sky of fog, with fog all round them, as if they were up in a balloon and hanging in the misty clouds.

> Simple statements are used again, increasing to two in the same sentence. This takes the idea further, looking down to the marshes and up to the hills.

> The first sentence or clause not to start with 'fog' really stands out.

GLOSSARY

aits – small islands in the middle of rivers
deified – turned into a god
cabooses – cooking rooms on ships' decks
collier-brigs – cargo ships that carried coal
rigging – masts, sails and ropes on sailing ships
gunwales – upper edges of the side of a ship
wards – administrative divisions of a city
'prentice – apprentice; someone learning a craft
parapet – barrier to prevent people falling over the edge
yards – long poles to support the bottom of ships sails

Language

Look closely at the comments Zack has made about the punctuation used in the second sentence of the extract.

> Uses a comma to separate the clause which adds further details about the river.

Fog up the river, where it flows among green aits and meadows; fog down the river, where it rolls deified among the tiers of shipping and the waterside pollutions of a great (and dirty) city.

> Uses a semi-colon to link the clause about the fog up the river with the clause about the fog down the river.

1   Working with a partner, make a list of the different ways the writer has used punctuation in this text. Discuss the effect the punctuation used had on you as a reader. Did the way the sentences were punctuated help you to build up a picture of the setting?

2   Working with a partner, find a similar descriptive passage from a contemporary novel. Compare the way the punctuation is used in the modern text and the differences from the *Bleak House* extract.

3   Now write your own description of a place you know well on a very wet day. Try to use the techniques used in the *Bleak House* extract you have just read and structure your sentences carefully in order to emphasise the effects of the weather. Use the skill steps from the previous sections.

Support

Think about how you can use punctuation to:
- link ideas using connectives or semi-colons,
  e.g. As the moon went down, the back gate creaked open; something moved in the darkness.
- add detail with subordinate clauses,
  e.g. Peering hard, I could only see the vague outlines of old flowerpots piled high by the fence and when I felt brave enough, I went a little closer, jumping with fear at the brush of a strand of ivy across my face.

Stretch

Use colons and semi-colons to help you build longer and more ambitious sentences. Try to add details that are specific and help your reader imagine a clear picture, as Dickens does when he is describing all the people and places that the fog affects. Think about the ways you can repeat sentence structures to help you create specific effects.

Apply your learning

Task You have been asked to write an article for a newspaper for young people providing advice and information for students on how to survive secondary school. This could be a serious article or a funny one, depending on the advice you want to give!

1   Firstly, create a plan showing what you could include in your article. In your plan, think about the ways in which you can present the information and advice you will give.

2   When you have completed your plan, draft your article. Remember to:

   ● use a variety of sentence shapes to create deliberate effects, including speech

   ● link your ideas and build up detail

   ● check that your punctuation is varied and that you are beginning to use more advanced punctuation, such as colons and semi-colons, in more complex sentence structures.

3   When you have completed your draft, use your proofreading and editing skills to review and revise your article. Make any necessary improvements in your final draft.

4   Finally, annotate your article to show evidence of how you have used punctuation and how you have constructed your sentences to create deliberate effects.

Assess to Progress

Look at the writing you have just completed and use it to assess your progress in the skills you have been practising. Rate yourself again for each skill.

● I have used full stops, capital letters, commas, apostrophes, question marks and exclamation marks accurately.

● I know when I should use semi-colons and colons and have used these correctly.

● I am confident when punctuating speech.

● I have structured my sentences carefully to create deliberate effects.

● I have proofread and edited my work.

Now answer the following questions

1   What have you learned that you did not know or could not do before?

2   What was the hardest part of this unit?

In your class, your friend has written an entire English essay in text message speak. The teacher said she couldn't understand a word of what the girl had written, but can you?

The essay started like this:

```
Sum teecherz r jst 2 borin n old fashioned & they need 2 b
up 2 date with wat goes on 2day. Dey shd chng, nt us kdz.
Of corz txt tlk shd b allowd in classes coz over thousands
of yrs r language as chngd plenty of times & teecherz shd
learn it 2.

My smmr hols wr CWOT. B4 we used 2go2 NY 2C my bro, his GF
& thr 3 :- kids FTF. ILNY, its a gr8 place.

But last year, we …
```

1   Rewrite the opening of the essay in complete, carefully punctuated sentences so that the teacher can understand it.

> **Hint**
>
> **In case you're stuck!**
> **CWOT** – complete waste of time
> **NY** – New York
> **GF** – girlfriend
> **:-** – screaming
> **FTF** – face to face
> **ILNY** – I love New York

2   Add two paragraphs describing your own summer holiday. Make sure you use a range of punctuation to help your readers understand what you have written.

Progress in ... Improving vocabulary for precision and impact

LEARNING OBJECTIVES

- Use vocabulary to create considered and appropriate effects.
- Draw independently on the range and variety of your own vocabulary to choose words appropriate to purpose and audience.
- Use a range of strategies and resources to extend your vocabulary choices.

Activate your learning

Jake has written the following passage about the first time he explored caves with a professional team. He has tried to use interesting words, but his teacher has underlined some phrases and asked him to find one word that means the same as the phrase .

We went to Cheddar Gorge early that morning. It was <u>windy and rainy</u> outside, so I thought it would be <u>warmer and more dry</u> inside. The cliffs of the Gorge <u>rise fearfully high</u> above each side of the valley and the sun was just beginning to <u>appear and rise</u> over the tops of the cliffs that <u>were all around us</u>. We were going to <u>check out and explore</u> Gough's cave first.

Gough's cave is <u>both scary and awesome</u> because it was where the body of Cheddar Man was found in 1903. Cheddar Man is the oldest skeleton ever found in Britain that hadn't been <u>broken up</u>. Rumour has it that he died a <u>fierce and cruel</u> death, and some say that he was <u>eaten alive by other humans</u>! He was <u>discovered</u> with <u>a lot of</u> other bones in a <u>big pile</u> that had all been <u>carved and cut up</u>. Knowing this body and these bones had been discovered here, it filled me with <u>fear and dread</u>, even though <u>I knew there was no reason for my worries</u>.

1 Using a thesaurus and dictionary, work with a partner to decide on one or two words that you could use instead of each of the underlined phrases. Make sure they have the same meaning. You might need to put your new word somewhere else in the sentence.

e.g. 'even though I knew there was no reason for my worries' could become 'even though my worries **were pointless**'

2 Join with another pair and discuss why your new word choices are better than Jake's original ones.

Jake has tackled the next paragraph by himself, using a thesaurus to help him make better word choices. However, when he gives his work to his teacher, she tells him it doesn't make any sense! She has underlined some of the words that she thinks Jake needs to look at.

> We started at the Black Cat cave. It was <u>caliginous</u> inside and it felt as if the world outside had <u>discontinued</u>. We had a <u>facile</u> climb to Mushroom Chamber and then we had to <u>squirm</u> into Sand Chamber. After that, we <u>plummeted</u> down a steel ladder into Boulder chamber.

3 a) Working with a partner, use a dictionary to check what the underlined words mean and then explain why they do not make the best sense.

b) Choose a more appropriate word that Jake could use for each of the underlined words. Use a dictionary to check the word's meaning and make sure it makes sense in the text.

Assess to Progress

How well can you use vocabulary already? Do you think about the type of text you are writing and choose words carefully to fit this? Can you choose vocabulary to create appropriate effects for your readers? Thinking about recent writing you have done, rate yourself for each skill below, deciding where you fit best on the scale. Find evidence to back up your decision.

| 1 | 3 | 4 | 5 | 6 | 7 |

I find this difficult.   I'm getting there.   I'm good at this.

- I can use vocabulary to create considered and appropriate effects.

  Self-check: Do you think about what the words you have chosen suggest to your reader and you can use words to create the effect?

- I can draw independently on my own vocabulary to choose words appropriate to purpose and audience.

  Self-check: Do you think about who is reading your work and think about what effect you want to have on them? Do you choose words that suit your purpose for writing?

- I can use different strategies and resources to extend my vocabulary.

  Self-check: Can you use a thesaurus and dictionary to find appropriate words or change part of a word you already know so that it makes sense, e.g. you can make 'happy' into 'happiness'.

Build your skills

Writers can choose words that are not just 'right', but that also suggest particular things to the reader.

1 Read the extract below from a Friends of the Earth leaflet. As you read, think about how the writer has made the charity seem positive through the choice of words. Working with a partner, answer the questions around the text to help you explore the vocabulary used.

a) The writer has used superlative adjectives to make the charity sound like it is the best at what it does. What other words could have been used instead?

Friends of the Earth is:

• the UK's most influential environmental campaigning organisation

• the most extensive environmental network in the world, with almost one million supporters across five continents and 70 national organisations worldwide

• a unique network of campaigning local groups, working in over 220 communities throughout England, Wales and Northern Ireland

• dependent on individuals for 90 per cent of its income

b) Why do you think the writer repeats the word 'environmental'?

c) Why do you think the writer has used numbers? What is the purpose of doing this?

d) What words can you think of that mean the same as 'unique'? Make a list of five other words or phrases that mean the same thing.

2 a) Now read the text opposite, which is taken from the Greenpeace website. As you read, decide what the purpose of this text is – what does the writer want the reader to think?

   b) Find examples of words that you think the writer has chosen specifically to achieve this purpose.

A **suffix** is a syllable added to the end of a word to modify its meaning. The writer of the Greenpeace website opposite, has taken the verbs 'contaminate', 'eliminate' and 'protect' and added the suffix '-ion' to change them into nouns.

3 a) What overall effect does the use of these words have on you as a reader? Choose the statement below that you most agree with and explain why.

   ● It makes the problems seem bigger and the solutions more important.

   ● It makes you think that it affects everyone.

   ● It makes you feel that the writer is trying to impress you.

b) Find other verbs in the text that you could change into nouns using the '-ion' suffix. What effect would this create?

GREENPEACE

GREENPEACE

➤ **HOME**

▸ About Greenpeace

▸ What we do

▸ Greenpeace victories

▸ Blogs

▸ Get involved

▸ Donate

▸ Greenpeace News

▸ Work for Greenpeace

▸ Discussion forum

▸ Photos and audio & video

▸ Reports

Our goal is to ensure the ability of the earth to nurture life in all its diversity. We organise public campaigns:

- for preventing climate change by ending our addiction to polluting fuels and promoting clean, renewable and efficient energy
- for the protection of oceans and ancient forests
- for the elimination of toxic chemicals
- against the release of genetically modified organisms into nature
- for nuclear disarmament and an end to nuclear contamination.

Reinforce your skills

It is important to choose the right vocabulary for the kind of writing you are doing. When you are expressing opinions or making comparisons, you need to use **superlative** and **comparative** adjectives.

You could use **superlative** adjectives when reviewing a TV programme, recounting an experience or giving instructions:

That was the most **amazing** Doctor Who episode I have ever seen.

The **greatest** holiday I ever had was when I went to Italy.

The **best** way to get there is by taking the next left.

We make superlative adjectives by adding 'most' in front of the existing adjective or by adding the suffix '-est' to the existing adjective. Some irregular adjectives such as 'good' and 'bad' change into new words in their superlative form, e.g. 'best' and 'worst'.

Comparative adjectives are used to compare two things. You could use comparative adjectives when writing up the results of an experiment in science or when recommending a holiday destination or a new car:

Solution X produced a **greater** amount of acid than solution Y.

Eurodisney is more **suitable** for families with young children than Ibiza.

The Zonda is **better** than the Ferrari.

We make comparative adjectives by adding 'more' in front of the existing adjective or by adding the suffix '-er' to the existing adjective. Some irregular adjectives such as 'good' or 'bad' change into new words in their comparative form, e.g. 'better' and 'worse'

1   Work with a partner to decide how you would make the superlative and comparative versions of the following adjectives:

bright	**fast**	**high**
beautiful	**comfortable**	**happy**
many	**clean**	**ancient**

2   a)   Join with another pair to make a group of four. In your group, think of three films or DVDs you have all watched this year. Spend five minutes comparing the films and discussing which you enjoyed the most.

   b)   Working on your own write a paragraph for the DVD review page of the school magazine comparing the films you discussed and recommending your favourite. Think about the comparative and superlative adjectives you use.

   c)   Compare your paragraph with a partner and discuss your choices of comparative and superlative adjectives and the reasons why you chose them.

3   What other types of writing do you think you would use comparative and superlative adjectives in? Look back at pieces of writing you have completed recently to try to find examples of these.

Extend your skills

When you are writing, it is important to select the words that most effectively help your reader to understand what you want to say and create the right effect in their minds. You need to keep the purpose and audience for your writing in mind to make sure you choose the right words.

Read the text on the opposite page. It is the first draft of an appeal from WaterAid, a charity that works to help the world's poorest people gain access to safe water and sanitation.

Language

WaterAid works in countries across Africa and Asia. We want to help overcome poverty by helping people gain access to good water. We work to give people the skills they need to understand why clean water is so important and to set up projects that help governments provide their people with clean water and sanitation. Everyone has a right to clean water because, without it, illness and disease can ruin a community. Also, people spend a long time gathering water every day instead of doing other things that would help them, like going to school. If people are ill a lot, it puts a burden on the rest of the community as well, meaning they can't do what they need to be doing.

> How can I improve the first sentence so it shows how WaterAid works?

> How can I stress how vital the work we do is?

> The word 'people' is repeated several times. How can I change some of these words to make it appealing?

> How can I convey the charity's and convince people to donate?

1   Working with a partner, look at the annotations and discuss how the writer could improve the vocabulary to create these effects.

2   Using the skills you have developed, rewrite the text, choosing vocabulary that helps to create the effects the writer wants to create.

Support

How can you make sure that the words you choose match the topic you are writing about? You could research the topic on the internet or look at the vocabulary that other charities use in their appeals.

Stretch

How could you change the vocabulary to persuade a younger reader that WaterAid does vital work? Think about the words you would need to change so they would be understood by a child.

3   When you have rewritten the appeal, write a brief commentary explaining the reasons for vocabulary choices you have made.

Apply your learning

Working on your own, you are now going to use the skills you have developed in this unit to help you to complete the task below.

Task You have been asked to write the text for two websites to inform people about the work of a charity called Monkey World.

The first web page is aimed at adults with an interest in conservation and should show that Monkey World is more than just a monkey park.

The second web page is aimed at teachers who want to educate their pupils by showing them animals in their natural conditions.

You have been given a limit of 200 words for each web page and the information below. You should choose vocabulary that will help your audience to see how vital and positive the work that goes on at Monkey World is. Remember to:

- choose words that are appropriate for the audience and topic
- use vocabulary that helps the reader to understand the work Monkey World does and that creates particular effects for the reader.

Monkey World is home to 150 different types of monkey.	It is the largest group of monkeys outside Africa.
It was set up in 1987.	It takes in circus animals, animals that have been used in experimentation and animals that have been pets.
It rescues monkeys used in the tourist industry in Spain and gives them a home.	The animals are taught to be social again and to be monkeys again, not people.
It works with governments.	There is specialist care for the monkeys.
It wants to stop trafficking of monkeys across the world.	The monkeys are given large spaces to live in.
It wants to stop monkeys being kept as pets.	More and more monkeys need rescuing each year.

Assess to Progress

How good are you now at choosing vocabulary to match the topic you are writing about and to create particular effects for your reader? Look at the writing you have just completed and rate yourself for each of the skills below.

1		3	4	5	6	7

I find this difficult.   I'm getting there.   I'm good at this.

- I can use vocabulary to create considered and appropriate effects.

- I can draw independently on the range and variety of my vocabulary to choose words appropriate to purpose and audience.

- I can use a range of strategies and resources to extend available vocabulary choices.

SKILLS FOR LIFE

You want to raise some extra money quickly and have decided to sell some of your old things. Your parents have said that if you write out the advertisement, they will add the things you are selling to an online marketplace for you.

Write an advertisement for one of your items. In your ad, you need to use vocabulary that is clear, simple and accurate so that people who might be interested in buying the item can understand your advertisement easily. You should include the following details:

- A headline of no more than eight words. This is the headline for your advertisement which will be listed on the main page of the online marketplace, e.g. Lost DVDs – Boxed Set Series 2

- A statement of no more than 100 words that describes the item you are selling. In this statement you need to give more details about what you are selling, choosing vocabulary that will inform and persuade readers. Make sure in your description of the item that you include the reasons why someone should buy it.

Progress in ... Reviewing spelling

- Use your knowledge of spelling rules and spelling strategies when working on your own.
- Spell correctly most words that are made up of a lot of syllables, including some tricky or unfamiliar words.
- Use your skills in editing and proofreading to improve the accuracy of your spelling.

Activate your learning

Check out your spelling skills as you work in pairs to play each of these one-minute games.

1 Read through the following text in pairs. As you read, take it in turns to spot a spelling mistake. You score one point for each mistake you spot and another point for each word you can change so that it is spelt correctly. You score a bonus point if you can explain to your partner how you know the word is misspelt and another bonus point if you can explain how to work out what the correct spelling should be.

> Allthough their are many successfull films being made the film industery is suffring becoz they are often pirated. Theirfore a new gadjit which finds and blinds camras that are illegaly filming in cinemas should be very poplar. You need to rember that it will take some time before it is wildly availabul. However the results are already encourageing sinse the gadjit is able to shoot a streem of white light into the camera witch spoils the qualitty of the pirated film. It won't take to long for the crimnals to reelize what is happning. Infact a lot of pirateing could just dissappear overnight.

2   How many words can you build by adding one or more of the prefixes and/or suffixes below to one of the root words in red? Score a point for each new word you can create.

Root words:	decide	fame	fine	employ	complete
Prefixes:	de-	pre-	in-	un-	re-
Suffixes:	-ly	-ing	-ed	-ous	-ion

3   Make a poster showing different spelling strategies you have used successfully in the past to help you learn to spell tricky words, e.g. necessary, beautiful, defining, occasionally, conscience, embarrassment, separate.

Assess to Progress

How good are you at making sure you spell correctly the words you use in your writing? Do you proofread carefully to make sure that you catch any spelling mistakes you make? For each of the skills below decide where you are on this scale.

1	2	3	4	5	6	7

I find this difficult.   I'm getting there.   I'm good at this.

●   I can spell words that are made up of many syllables and some really tricky ones,

   Self-check: Can you spell the following words without help? Accommodation, conscious, February. Close your book and practise spelling them.

●   I know and use spelling rules to help me remember how to spell longer words, e.g. Drop the "e" when you add -ing' to write: *writing* not *writeing*.

   Self-check: Were you able to work out the correct spellings for game 1? How easily could you explain how you spotted mistakes? How well did you score in game 2?

●   I know a number of different ways to learn and remember how to spell tricky words and I can choose and use the best one to help me.

   Self-check: Can you break a word up into sounds or syllables to help you remember all its parts? e.g. re – mem – ber ✓ not rember ✗

●   I remember to check my spellings when I've written my first draft of a text and then check them again after writing my final draft.

   Self-check: When proofreading your work, do you always check the spelling of any tricky words using a dictionary?

Build your skills

To get even better at writing texts with correct spelling you need to pause before you write a word whose spelling you know you find tricky. You should then use the spelling rules and strategies you have already learned to help you work out how to spell it.

Study the flow diagram below that shows you how to do this, then try out the games in the next section to help you practise these skills.

Step 1 Question check

Oh no, I've got to write ... ✈ I can't remember how to spell it so I'll use the four checking questions to help me work it out.

Does it belong to a word family?	*I don't think so.*
Can I break the word up into syllables?	*Yes and I know how to spell 'plane' but not the part of the word that comes before it.*
Is there a spelling rule I remember that will help me?	*No.*
Is it made up of a root word + a prefix or + a suffix?	*Yes it's 'plane, + a prefix.*
What do I know about the prefix/suffix/root? Is the prefix likely to be spelt 'airo' + 'plane'?	*No, that doesn't look right.*
I wonder if it comes from Greek or Latin instead. What about spelling it 'aero' – like 'aerobics'?	***Aeroplane** – it looks right. I'll try that.*

Support

A **prefix** is a group of letters that fix onto the front of a root word and change its meaning, e.g. *mis + understood = misunderstood*, *which means the opposite of 'understood'*. When you add a prefix you don't need to change it or the root word.

A **suffix** is a group of letters that fix onto the end of a root word and tell the reader what job the word is doing, e.g. *quick + ly*. When '-ly' is added to a word it usually means it is doing the job of a describing word such as the adverb 'quickly' in the sentence 'He ran down the road quickly.'

Step 2   Strategy check'

> I need to learn how to spell aeroplane so I don't struggle with it next time. How will I remember it is aero + plane?

Which part of the word is hard to remember?	The **ae** at the start.
Which strategies can I use to help me remember this?	**Strategy 1:** *'Aero' comes from the Greek word for air and there are other words that begin with 'aer-', e.g. aerosol, aerobics, aerial.* **Strategy 2:** *It has the same vowels starting 'aero' that are in 'plane' so it's* **ae**roplane **Strategy 3:** *I'll write it in my spelling journal and use Look – say – cover – write – check.*

Reinforce your skills

Which words are you good at spelling and which ones do you know you find tricky?

1   Search through some of your recent work and make a list of ten tricky words you can spell and ten words you still struggle to spell and need to learn. If you can't find ten tricky words, you could work with these instead:

accommodation	**targeting**	**palettes**	**conscientiously**	**environmentally**
manoeuvre	**onomatopoeia**	**miniature**	**parliament**	**prejudice**

2   Work in a group.

a) First, take it in turns to be a spelling expert and share your knowledge.
    Spelling expert: Pick two tricky words you know how to spell and explain to your group how you managed to master them. Your method may help someone else!

b) Working together, take this spelling challenge.
    Spelling challenge: Can everyone in your group learn their ten tricky spellings? Use the list of spelling strategies below to help each other learn the correct spellings. Then work with a partner to test each other. Each word you spell correctly will earn a point for your group. The group with the highest overall score will be the winners!

Spelling strategies:
- Decide whether the word belongs to a word family. If so, what are the other members and how are they spelt? What is different? What is the same? e.g. *accommodate – accommodating*

- Break the word into its syllables, e.g. *ac-com-mo-da-tion* and underline the parts that are tricky to remember.

- Decide whether the word is made up of a root word + a prefix and/or a suffix. If it is, then write down the root word and the suffix and/or prefix. Decide whether there is a spelling rule for adding each prefix or suffix and, if there is, write it down,
  e.g. *root word = accommodate, suffix = -ion*
  Rule: to add the suffix -ion you need to lose the 'e' at the end of the root word.

- Make a list of spelling rules you already know that can help you learn to spell that word. Pick a strategy from the poster that you made earlier which you can use to help you remember each spelling.

Extend your skills

When you have finished drafting your writing you need to **proofread** it to check for spelling mistakes and edit it to make corrections. Proofreading can also help you to find opportunities to use more effective words.

When checking a first draft, read the text aloud (in your head or to a partner). Then read the text backwards, word by word. Search for any words that don't look right or you are unsure of and, if you are allowed, use a spell-checker or dictionary to check the spelling. **Remember to:**

- Highlight any words that you know you find tricky and use the spelling challenge to help you check them if you haven't got a dictionary.

- Check for homophones: words that sound the same but are spelt differently when they mean different things, e.g. 'their'/'there'/'they're'. Have you used the right one each time?

1 a) Use this approach to find and correct ten spelling mistakes in the text below.

> When you want to complane about somthing going on in the country it's worth writeing to you're Member of Parliaiment. There adress is available on the web or in the phonebook. Their going to lissen becos they want people living in there area to vote four them.

b) Now write the next paragraph of the text explaining another way to complain about an issue in the news that you feel strongly about. Then proofread it for spelling mistakes and edit it to correct any errors.

When proofreading, you should also investigate whether there are any words that you could replace with more effective vocabulary. Use your spelling challenge skills to help you work out how to spell the new word – then dare to use it!

2 Try to replace five words in the text you corrected in activity 1 a) with more effective words.

Stretch

Be a word gatherer. Try to spot words that work well in texts you are reading and dare to try them out in your own work.

Apply your learning

You are now going to use the skills you have developed through the unit to help you to complete the task below.

Task Choose an issue that you think the government should do something about. You could use one of the suggestions below.

- The way a group of people in society are treated.
- How pollution or waste can be reduced to help the environment.
- How facilities for young people in your area can be improved.

Write a letter to the Prime Minister explaining the problem and telling him what you would like the government to do. Try to choose the most effective words to help persuade him and make sure you spell these correctly.

Choose a planning format to help you to organise your ideas and then write the first draft of your letter. When you have written your first draft, you should proofread and edit it to show that you can:

- spell difficult words correctly
- spot and correct any misspelt words
- improve the vocabulary you use by choosing more appropriate words.

As you review your first draft, underline or highlight the changes you need to make. Then write the final version of your letter.

Assess to Progress

How good are you at spelling and proofreading now? Look at the letter you have just written and use it to assess your progress in the skills you have been practising. For each of the skills below decide where you fit best on this scale.

1	2	3	4	5	6	7

I find this difficult.   I'm getting there.   I'm good at this.

- I can spell words that are made up of many syllables and some really tricky ones.

- I know and use spelling rules to help me remember how to spell longer words.

- I know a number of different ways to learn and remember how to spell tricky words and I can choose and use the best one to help me.

- I remember to check my spellings when I have written my first draft of a text and then check it again after writing my final draft to spot and correct the spelling mistakes in it.

SKILLS FOR LIFE

Your local newspaper has announced that your nearest leisure centre is to close down because it is not used enough and is becoming too expensive to run. Write a letter to the editor of your local newspaper explaining:

- why having a leisure centre is important to people in your community

- what could be done to encourage local people to make more use of it

- how the leisure centre could make more money.

When you write your letter, take care to think about the way you spell the words you use. As you want your views to be taken seriously, it is important to sound as mature as you can so try to use more sophisticated words and work out how they should be spelt.

Remember to check your spelling when you have written your first draft and to proofread the letter again when you have written your final version.

Writing
Assessing your Progress

TARGETS FOR PROGRESS

- Experiment with language to develop a sense of character.
- Choose details to recount events in an entertaining way.

Working through this unit will give you the opportunity to show the progress you have made in your writing skills. You will have the chance to bring together the skills you developed in the earlier writing units as you prepare for a writing task that will assess how well you can create an entertaining account.

Activate your learning

In this unit you will use language techniques to create a vivid picture of someone you know well. One technique you will use is figurative language. This is when writers use words to create pictures in the reader's mind. One way writers do this is by using comparisons like similes and metaphors.

- **Simile:** a simile is a comparison that uses 'like' or 'as',

    e.g. 'he saw a filthy one-eyed face as rough as bark'.

    The description 'rough as bark' makes the reader imagine tough skin that is wrinkled in deep, twisted lines and isn't smooth to touch.

- **Metaphor:** a metaphor makes a comparison by saying something is something else,

    e.g. 'And still the wind blew: pelting their faces with tiny darts of ice ...

    This description compares the freezing snow with 'darts' made from ice. A dart is hard and sharp so this would be painful.

1   Think of a suitable comparison to complete the simile and metaphor in this sentence:

    e.g. Torak stared into a face as hard as ... The beard was a ...

2   Compare your sentence with a partner's and explain the effect you were trying to create with your choice of words.

Progress task

Write about an event involving one of your friends, which shows what sort of person they are and creates a vivid picture of them so that the producers of the TV programme can appreciate their potential entertainment value.

1 Answer these questions to identify useful information in the task:

- **Audience:** who will read your writing?

- **Form:** what type of writing are you being asked to do?

- **Purpose:** What are you trying to achieve in your writing?

2 Now look at your task in more detail. Read the information below and identify what new details it gives you.

Are you and your friends the people we're looking for?

Channel X is looking for a group of friends to spend a week at an outdoor pursuits centre in Scotland. We need people with good personalities who viewers would enjoy watching as they have a go at a range of activities such as orienteering, rock-climbing, canoeing and pot-holing.

Interested?

All you have to do is write to us and tell us a story involving one or more of your friends, which clearly shows what sort of person he/she is and which creates a really vivid picture of him/her.

Some suggestions:

○ Decide what aspects of your friend's personality and behaviour would make viewers want to watch them.

○ Try to think of an incident which really brings out this aspect of your friend's character.

○ Create as vivid a picture as you can of your friend by including some, or all, of the following:

 – A description of what they look like: physical features, style, mannerisms, gait, and so on

 – What they say and how they say it: tone, pace, vocal mannerisms

 – How they think of themselves: self-confidence

 – What other people think and say about them: those who know them well and those who don't.

GLOSSARY

gait – the way someone walks

Build your skills

1 Using the information you have been given, start planning your ideas for your application to take part in the show. You could use the following headings to organise your ideas:

● Personality and behaviour.

● An event that shows what my friend is like.

● Details about how my friend looks and talks.

Tip: You could always make up a friend if you don't want to use a real one!

Writers use interesting details and **figurative language** to create vivid descriptions and make comparisons that are not literal. The purpose of this is to interest the reader by providing a new way of looking at things.

Read the example of descriptive writing on the following page called *My Mother*.

2 For each of the following examples of figurative language, explain what image the comparison makes you think of:

● 'a pair of knotted-string legs' gives me an image of legs that are ...

● 'mountain of overflowing carrier bags' makes me visualise ...

● 'the look of a dandelion seed-head' makes me imagine she looks ...

3 How could you use similes and metaphors to make your description of your friend more vivid?

4 Writing to entertain and describe will also have other features. Working with a partner, look again at the extract opposite and find another example of each of these features:

Feature	Example 1	Example 2
Past tense for narrative	'... **made** me think that my mother was not really on top of the situation'	
Present tense for introducing character	Her head always **seems** to be pushed forward'	
Well-chosen detail	'A small head, framed by wispy strands of hair that refuse all attempts at control ...'	
Dialogue that reveals character	'People are absolutely fascinating, Jane! They teach you so much!'	
Extended noun phrase	'Young, inquisitive ostrich'	

Extended noun phrase

My mother always reminds me of a young, inquisitive ostrich. It's not just that she's tall, it's the overall shape created by an elongated, slim upper body and a pair of knotted-string legs separated by a large middle portion. A small head, framed by wispy strands of hair that refuse all attempts at control, and a pair of rather large feet, complete the picture.

Figurative language

Well-chosen detail

Her head always seems to be pushed forward, as if trying to get a better look at something. This is because she usually is: her very clear, very blue eyes are short-sighted and she's always losing her glasses; but it's also because she takes such an intense interest in just about anything and everything. Some of my friends say that when they first met her they felt like they were under interrogation, but then they came to realise that she was just interested – in them, their families, in what they do, think, everything! 'People are absolutely fascinating, Jane! They teach you so much!'

Dialogue that reveals character

She's really embarrassing to be with, sometimes, because she talks to anyone – and this is why I arrived home last week and found a 'bag-lady' drinking tea in our kitchen.

'This is Annie – she's just having a cup of tea while we think about where she could spend the night!' announced my mother in response to the look of horror on my face as I took in the mountain of overflowing carrier bags, and the twitching of my nose as it tried to identify the unfamiliar smell. The over-bright tone, and the way even more strands of hair than usual seemed to have escaped, giving her the look of a dandelion seed-head, made me think that my mother was not really on top of the situation.

Figurative language

'I'm just going to help Jane get started on her homework, Annie – won't be a minute!' she trilled, sounding like one of those really phoney mothers they have in situation comedies on the television, while propelling me very firmly back through the kitchen door and into the living room.

Past tense for narrative

GLOSSARY

inquisitive – curious, enquiring
elongated – long, extended

Language

> ## Support
>
> An **extended noun phrase** means a noun that has had more information added to it. In this example, 'ostrich' has two adjectives before it ('young' and 'inquisitive') to expand the detail and make the image clearer for the reader. Sometimes details like this can be added after the noun, e.g. 'an ostrich with a long neck and a sense of curiosity'.

> ## Stretch
>
> Talk with a partner about the effect of the examples you have found of well-chosen details, and extended noun phrases.

5 Write a paragraph to describe Annie. **Remember:** use present tense to introduce the character and include at least one example of:

● well-chosen detail ● extended noun phrases ● figurative language.

> ## Support
>
> Look at the following plan for a description of Annie. Use these details and develop them to help you write your paragraph.
>
>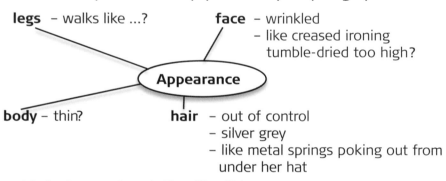
>
> **legs** – walks like ...?
>
> **face** – wrinkled
> – like creased ironing tumble-dried too high?
>
> **Appearance**
>
> **body** – thin?
>
> **hair** – out of control
> – silver grey
> – like metal springs poking out from under her hat
>
> You could start your description like this:
> *Annie is homeless but looks like a typical granny. Her wrinkled face is ...*

6 When you have completed and checked your paragraph, highlight the features you have used. You should:

● tick each present tense verb

● underline a well-chosen detail

● draw a circle around an extended noun phrase

● put a box around any examples of figurative language.

7 a) Swap your paragraph with a partner. Check that they have annotated their ideas accurately. Choose one statement from the ideas column and one statement from the vocabulary column that you think best describes their paragraph. Select an example to support each statement.

Ideas	Vocabulary
Relevant ideas are developed with some imaginative detail.	Vocabulary is chosen to make the description entertaining to read.
Some ideas are developed in detail.	Some vocabulary has been deliberately chosen to make the text entertaining.
There are some relevant ideas with a little detail given.	Vocabulary is simple with an attempt to use words for effect.

b) Look again at your own work. What could you improve when you write about your friend for the TV programme?

Reinforce your learning

1 You are now going to read the rest of the extract from *My Mother*. Working with a partner, explore how it uses the features of writing to recount and describe by answer the annotated questions.

'What's going on?' I demanded as my mother closed the door behind us and collapsed onto the sofa.

'Don't ask!' she said – then proceeded to tell me.

a) What does this detail tell us about the mother's attitude to the 'Annie problem'?

b) Which tense is used here? Why?

Apparently, my mother had arrived home from work to find Annie sitting on our front doorstep, in the rain, surrounded by her collection of bags, and crying.

'Well I couldn't just step over her and ignore her, could I?' pleaded my mother.

c) What does the way the mother speaks tell us about her and her relationship with her daughter?

Which is why she had brought her in for a cup of tea and listened to her tale of woe, which, as far as my mother could make out basically came down to her having nowhere to spend the night – 'though she doesn't seem to have a very secure grip on reality – and her sense of distant past and recent past seems a bit confused, I must admit,' remarked my mother, absent-mindedly winding a loose thread around her finger as she tried to make sense of Annie's rambling tale.

'I've made all sorts of suggestions and phoned every department I can think of that might have some sort of responsibility for situations like this and, well, I can't find anybody to take any responsibility. It really is a terrible state of affairs ...'

Before she could get on her soapbox about social responsibility, I cut in.

'So what are you going to do?'

'The thing is,' she replied, 'she seems to think that because I asked her in, she can stay here ...' her voice tailed off and she looked at me questioningly, as if she was hoping that I would say that was a marvellous idea, absolutely no problem whatsoever!

'Dad'll go mad,' I said.

d) Which tense is used here? Explain why.

As the faint, desperate gleam of hope faded from her eyes, we both heard a door slam. 'That'll be him!' she gasped.

e) What does this detail tell us about the mother?

My father is a lovely, patient man – very caring, but he thinks that some of my mother's 'projects' as he calls them, go beyond what he can reasonably be expected to agree to; I think this could be one of those 'projects'. And looking at my mother's expression as she leapt up off the sofa, I think even she recognised that fact.

'You see to Annie,' she hissed, 'I'll talk to him!'

f) What image does this metaphor give of the daughter at this point in the story?

And she launched herself through the door, leaving me doing an impersonation of a stranded goldfish. However, I knew I couldn't just abandon her, so I followed her into the hall only to find her with the front door open, staring after our visitor as she shuffled down the drive.

g) Why is this detail appropriate to describe Annie?

'But Annie! Where will you stay?' she called.

h) What does this dialogue reveal about the relationship between the mother and the daughter?

'Mum! Leave it!' I growled, dragging her back inside before Annie could change her mind. 'Just be thankful for a lucky escape!'

'Yes. Yes, I suppose you're right. But, you know, the camp bed ...'

At that point, luckily, we heard dad's car.

'You're right, of course,' she said, holding open the front door for dad.

'I've just passed a really sad case at the end of the road,' he said, getting out of the car. 'An old dear with a stack of carrier bags. I wonder where she's come from.'

'Mmm. I wonder. Poor thing!'

Extend your learning

An important part of your application for the reality TV show is to think of an incident which really brings out your friend's personality. The writer of *My Mother* did this with the story about Annie. Look at this account of an incident involving a character called Helen.

> Finally catching sight of them, Helen thrust her arm into the air like an Olympic shot-putter about to throw, and bellowed to attract their attention. They, and the rest of the audience, turned just in time to see her as she belly-flopped onto the unsuspecting string section tuning up for the overture, having missed her footing as she strode across the corner of the orchestra pit.

1   Pick out an example of each of the following techniques used in this account:

   - figurative language
   - extended noun phrases
   - past tense for narrative
   - well-chosen details.

2   The writer of this account wants to improve it. What suggestions can you make? Discuss with a partner ways you could improve it and then rewrite the paragraph to include these improvements.

Progress task

Your task is to write about an event involving one of your friends, which clearly shows what sort of person they is and which creates a really vivid picture of them so that the producers of the TV programme can appreciate their potential entertainment value.

Look at the planning for *My Mother* on the next page:

1   Now spend a few minutes planning your own writing about an event involving one of your friends which clearly shows that they are suitable for the reality TV show. Use the ideas you recorded earlier in this unit and plan the best order for your ideas so that you introduce your friend and recount an event that she/he was involved in.

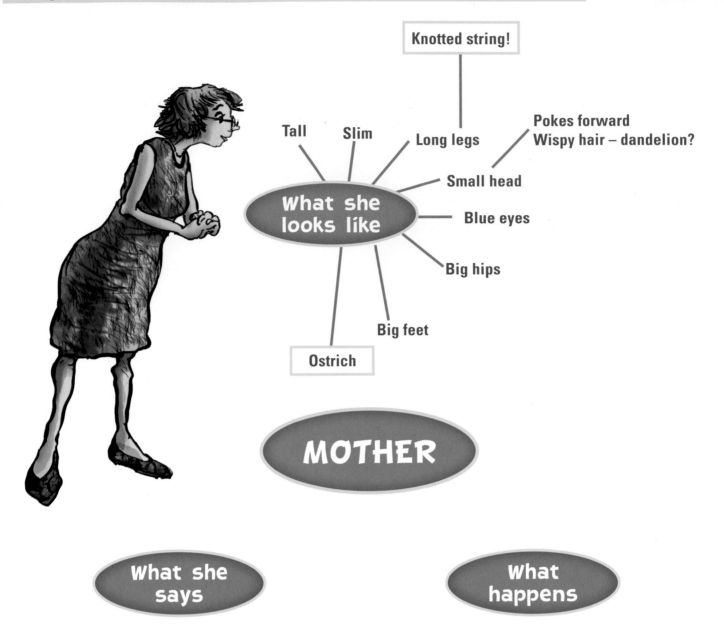

Knotted string!

Tall   Slim   Long legs   **Pokes forward**
Wispy hair – dandelion?

What she looks like

Small head

Blue eyes

Big hips

Big feet

Ostrich

MOTHER

What she says

What happens

tries to get daughter to understand / says how terrible it is for the old lady / reluctantly agrees with daughter / panics when husband returns

finds 'bag lady' on doorstep / invites her in / tries to help her / doesn't want to turn her away / knows husband and daughter won't let her stay / old lady leaves by herself

2 Use your plan, the checklist of writing features on page 228 and the *My Mother* text to help you write the reality show application and think about what you need to include. You have 30 minutes to complete this task. When you have finished, check that you have used all of the features, and correct any technical errors you find.

Assess to Progress

This unit has focused on the features of writing to describe and narrate an event. Read the example below and answer the questions.

I think that my friend, James Brown, should be a contestant on your new outdoor pursuit reality show. His being about 6ft it is funny to watch him try to take part in some events, such as canoeing where he can't even fit in the boat properly.

Anyway as you said a story must be included I've been putting a lot of thought into which hilarious story I could tell you. In the end I chose this one.

A couple of months ago James and I, along with a couple of mates, went to some local fields to have a game of football. We were playing and then the ball was kicked, accidentally, into some nearby bushes. Just below the bushes was a small river which James did not know about. We all went over to the bushes to retrieve it. I carefully slopped into the bushes and found the ball, I then grabbed it and climbed out. James then asked me for some strange reason whether I had got the ball, even though I was holding it. I sarcastically said no, and then to our utter amazement he dived into the bush as though he was rugby tackling one of the few trees amongst the bushes. We walked round to the side of the bush to see where he had fallen. We could see him hanging onto a thin, branch on the edge of the 7ft drop to the river. Slowly but surely the branch was going to eventually snap. As he was getting more worried, we were beginning to cry with laughter. Suddenly the branch snapped and he fell, SPLASH. He quickly scrambled out, soaking wet but now laughing too.

This is why I think James should be a contestant on your show, he is not the cleverest person in the world but he finds everything funny, even if it happens to him.

1   What features have been used well? How do you think the writer could improve the recount?

2   Now swap your own work with a partner's. Find examples of the following features in their writing. Choose one of the features and explain why you think it is effective. Then write a comment to explain what they could do to improve their writing.

   ● Past tense for narrative

   ● Present tense for introducing character

   ● Well-chosen detail

   ● Dialogue that reveals character

   ● Extended noun phrases

   ● Figurative language

3   Choose a statement from each column of the table on page 229 that you think best describes their writing.

Pearson Education
Edinburgh Gate
Harlow
Essex
CM20 2JE
© Pearson Education Limited 2008

Series Editor: Geoff Barton
Series Consultant: Michael Jones

The rights of Bernadette Carroll, Claire Austin-Macrae, Clare Constant, Emma Lee and Liz Lockwood to be identified as the authors of this work has been asserted by them in accordance with the Copyright, Design and Patents Act of 1988.

With many thanks to Chris Edge and John Green.

ISBN: 978-1-4058-7520-2
Second impression 2008